Marketing and the Library

Marketing and the Library

Gary T. Ford
Editor

The Haworth Press
New York

Marketing and the Library has also been published as *Journal of Library Administration,* Volume 4, Number 4, Winter 1983.

The Haworth Press, Inc., 28 East 22 Street, New York, NY 10010

Library of Congress Cataloging in Publication Data
Main entry under title:

Marketing and the library.

"Has also been published as Journal of library administration, volume 4, number 4, winter 1983"—T.p. verso.
Includes bibliographical references.
Contents: Introduction / Gary T. Ford—Megatrend marketing / Barbara Conroy—Library market segmentation / Anne J. Matthews—[etc.]
1. Public relations—Libraries. 2. Library administration. I. Ford, Gary T.
Z716.3.M287 1984   021.7   84-668
ISBN 0-86656-307-5

Marketing and the Library

Journal of Library Administration
Volume 4, Number 4

CONTENTS

> *A vision of possible futures represents a stimulus and guide for library administrators responsible for planning to meet—and create—the library future. "Megatrends" identified by Naisbitt reveal impacts now being felt by libraries and our society. Strategic planning together with marketing provide tools for shaping the library's response. Innovative marketing efforts can be based on megatrend impacts.*

> *Traditionally, libraries have attempted to serve everyone in the community with programs, services and materials which the library staff assumes will be useful and interesting to users. Market segmentation is the process of dividing up the community into homogeneous groups, and then developing unique programs for each of the target segments. This article discusses the concepts of undifferentiated, concentrated and differentiated marketing, various approaches to segmenting the market, and specific criteria for market segmentation. Library decision-makers will find market segmentation to be a useful tool for turning an indifferent general public into enthusiastic user groups.*

> *A marketing program is of little value if it is not implemented properly. Successful marketing programs recognize the need to position the library in the minds of the public and the staff; to balance demands with resources and reward performance.*

FROM THE EDITOR

The field of marketing is increasingly developing and transferring its theory and application to the non-profit sectors of our society. Our experience and literature in this regard are expanding, and we are beginning to see the impact of the marketing field on the administration of library and information service organizations. In addition to marketing literature generally aimed at non-profit administrators, more and more references may be identified which are specific to the library and information field and which appear in the library literature itself. For those of us who see promise in utilizing the best that marketing has to offer, these are encouraging signs.

Marketing as a field or as a concept is all too often misunderstood. Unfortunately, the misunderstanding frequently leans toward the aversive and engenders suspicion or outright rejection of it by many who might otherwise enjoy its benefits. I'll leave it to the experts to explain this resistance, but some of it must originate in the belief that marketing practices somehow have the capacity to exploit the consumer. The worst scenario is one of the consumers as victims who are manipulated into behaviors that serve others' interests but not their own. Another common view of marketing restricts its characterization to the field of advertising. Other definitions likely exist. The truth is that these are misleading ideas. Marketing can assume an intelligent and conscious public. Exploitation is both unnecessary and contraindicated as an approach. Also, the major beneficiary to any successful and well administered marketing program is, and should be, the public who are the recipients of the organization's products and services.

This special issue, in the context of other useful literature, should engender a broader, more accurate and most positive perspective on marketing. Hopefully it will encourage marketing applications and research in librarianship. Guest Editor Gary Ford has worked hard to generate papers that are interesting, useful, and informative. He is currently Chairperson in Marketing at the University of Maryland at College Park. In addition to his writing, teaching, and consultation to business and industry, Dr. Ford has worked directly with library administrators. For several years he has conducted marketing seminars and workshops in the

United States and Central America for public and academic librarians and for government managers of documentation and information agencies. I feel privileged that he undertook this work.

I extend my appreciation to Dr. Ford and to the authors who worked so hard to bring you this issue. Their work and the work of others to whom they refer can teach most of us something new about marketing in the library world. Let me also take this opportunity to encourage increased and continued contributions in this area.

John R. Rizzo

Introduction

At the outset I would like to make clear my perspective on the need for libraries to adopt modern marketing techniques. Libraries do not need to adopt marketing techniques to survive. The society will always have libraries as repositories of accumulated knowledge. However, I am convinced that libraries need to adopt marketing (and other business methodologies) to prosper. In my opinion it is much more likely that the battles most library administrators face for relatively scarce resources will intensify rather than diminish. The only hope that library administrators have of winning their fair share of those battles is to be able to demonstrate convincingly that the products and services of the library are being demanded by the public, that they are the best set of products and services that can be offered based on user needs, and that they are being offered efficiently. Unless library administrators can provide persuasive evidence that dollars invested in libraries are well-spent they will be faced with relatively declining budgets. Because adoption of techniques used by business organizations offers a partial solution to decisions concerned with the best use of scarce resources, I was pleased to have the opportunity to act as Guest Editor.

The experience of editing this special issue of the *Journal of Library Administration* was both challenging and frustrating. The challenge was in going through the process of being an editor, i.e., to seek out and encourage prospective authors to submit manuscripts, to work with the four authors whose manuscripts were accepted from among those submitted to shape and reshape their manuscripts, and to meet the (liberal) deadlines established by John Rizzo. The frustration stemmed from an inability to attract manuscripts which report the results of empirical research done in a library setting. I was not successful in getting marketing academics or marketing professionals to submit reports of surveys or experiments to the special issue. (I offer some speculations on the reasons for this, later.) Nonetheless the articles which were accepted discuss topics which are important and germane to librarians/information scientists and should be of benefit to professional librarians.

The article by Barbara Conroy summarizes the "megatrends" hypothesized by John Naisbitt in his popular book and suggests implications for each of these trends on the marketing activities of libraries. Anne Matthews discusses focusing on user needs through the process of market segmentation. Professor Matthews discusses the criteria for successful

3

segmentation strategies and the types of variables which traditionally are used by marketers in the profit and not-for-profit sectors. Dragon and Leisner tackle the problem of implementing marketing in libraries and provide suggestions as well as two case histories of libraries which were able to plan and implement successful marketing programs. Finally, Professor Weingand discusses the concept of distribution of the library's product and the types of innovation in distribution which are possible and which may become necessary for libraries to meet user needs. In addition to the four original articles, I have chosen to reprint perhaps the most famous marketing article ever written, ''Marketing Myopia'' by Professor Theodore Levitt of the Harvard Business School. Although it has been almost 20 years since this article was originally published it remains relevant today because it discusses fundamentals of successful marketing (fundamentals which I believe are particularly relevant for library administrators). All in all this set of five articles provides a good overview of some of the major issues that library managers must face.

The preceding comments described the contents of this special issue. The following comments concern my observations about the type of research which is needed to speed the adoption of marketing and marketing techniques by libraries.

Two concepts which are central to the study of new product introduction concern the notions of the product life cycle and the diffusion of innovations. Briefly, the product life cycle holds that all products and services go through a four stage life cycle: Introduction, Growth, Maturity and Decline. During the introduction stage sales (or usage) grows slowly because it takes time for information about the new product or service to diffuse through the population. If the product or service provides better value (utility) than substitute items the sales of the product will enter a period of rapid growth, until the market for the product matures and sales level off. Eventually, as new products are developed which provide better value, sales decline. In order to prevent maturity from leading to decline organizations generally will attempt to modify the product so it remains competitive or offer it to new potential users.

The product life cycle has direct relevance to libraries. Based on the description provided above it is clear that most of the products and services offered by libraries are neither in the introduction or growth stage heading for decline. Conversely the use of marketing by libraries is probably in the latter state of introduction. That is, the word is getting around that marketing techniques and strategies can be used by libraries to help in the design of a product and service mix which does a better job meeting user needs and to assist in developing appropriate communications approaches to make this known to current and potential users, but there does not appear to have been rapid growth in the numbers of libraries actually using marketing strategies effectively.

From my perspective the question now is "How can the use of marketing by libraries be moved into the growth stage of its life cycle?" There are no easy, automatic answers to this question. However, I think we are past the point of merely talking (or writing) about how marketing can and should be used by libraries. The next step forward in the adoption of marketing by libraries will not come unless the literature begins to include empirical evidence from experiments, surveys or case histories. Librarians are going to demand evidence that marketing approaches are effective and will want to see what the likely problems are that they will face when adopting marketing strategies. This is especially true considering the negative perception that many librarians have about marketing. (Why should it be expected that any library administrator will devote scarce resources to an approach which is essentially untested in the library field when he or she is not comfortable with the idea of having to market anyway?)

Empirical studies cannot be reported if they are not conducted. So, suppose a library administrator is intrigued with the notion of developing and implementing a marketing program; where can this person go for help? The only two realistic options are consulting firms or universities.

I am not going to discuss that search process other than to state that either consultants or academics will have to be rewarded for helping the library. However, unlike consultants, academics can often be rewarded by the opportunity to publish research results.

In sum, the extent to which libraries will use marketing techniques is unclear. I am convinced marketing methods can assist libraries in doing a better job of allocating scarce resources and attracting new ones. But the widespread use of marketing techniques by libraries will not occur until reports of the experiences that libraries have had developing and implementing marketing programs begin to appear in the literature. Some library administrators will have to take the plunge.

Gary T. Ford, Guest Editor
College Park, Maryland

Megatrend Marketing:
Creating the Library's Future

Barbara Conroy

> The future is not a result of choices among alternative paths offered
> by the present, but a place that is created—created first in mind and
> will, created next in activity. The future is not some place we are
> going to, but one we are creating. The paths to it are not found but
> made, and the activity of making them changes both the maker and
> the destination—*John Schaar*

We ARE makers of our future. We build our future by what we
create— or do not create—in the present. Constructing our present builds
the route to our future. In effect, the future of libraries—whether they will
exist, what they will do and how they will do it—requires that we manage
and market today's libraries successfully. Thus, today's library managers
are prime contractors, building our collective library future based on their
view of what is possible and probable. The planning activities and actions
taken by today's managers affect not only their own libraries but the field
of librarianship.

Universally, library managers perceive their planning function as
essential for their library's survival. Short range planning is second
nature for most managers, prompted by daily problems and occasional
crises. As perceptive managers plan and decide and act, they see direct
impact as those plans, decisions and actions shape not only the present
nature of their library but also its future capabilities.

Planning drives the library as an organization, defines its mission,
develops its personnel and determines if and how the clientele's information needs will be met. Most planning (and its implementation) impacts
the future. Short range planning deals with today's issues, reacts for the
present. In contrast, long range planning focuses on conceptual frame-
works and institutional directions for the future. Central to long range
planning is the ability to plot change and anticipate its speed and potential
consequence for the organization. Thus, aware managers develop long
range vision knowing their decisions now will affect the organization's
structure, potential and people well into the future.

Barbara Conroy is an educational and library consultant living in Tabernash, Colorado. She has
published and consulted widely and is a regular column editor for *Journal of Library Administration*.

To plan effectively and to deliberately create for the future, however, library administrators need guides, especially for envisioning the future. Valuable perspectives from future oriented visionaries can help. Alvin Toffler is one. His *Future Shock* (1971) and *Third Wave* (1980) describe detailed chronicles of future possibilities. More recent is John Naisbitt's *Megatrends: Ten New Directions Transforming Our Lives* (1982). Megatrends presents a concise (some call it simplistic) and determinedly optimistic overview of major strategic trends and directions that hold significant implications for our lives, our work and our society.

Both Toffler and Naisbitt help us conceive not only the tremendous changes likely, but also their astounding scope and pace. For managers wanting to prepare for the future, a realistic perspective of the degree and speed of change is, perhaps, more important than the details of their visions. Even so, their substantive analysis of present trends and reasoned conjecture about future possibilities carry implications library administrators can ill afford to ignore as they seek viable library directions.

The weight of this responsibility and the difficulties implied are alarming to many of us. Personally and societally, individuals find periods of tremendous change disturbing. Both Naisbitt and Toffler address this but underscore how, even so, such times produce great sources of energy and ideas and re-direction. Transition periods offer enhanced opportunities for those who seek change, giving change agents' efforts added impetus since their influence and leverage is much greater then than during more stable times. Thus, the impact of managerial decisions is even more powerful. Their influence within professions and organizations is more likely to be pivotal. Serious-minded conjecture about the future deserves to be a factor in a manager's planning, particularly that for the long range.

Consequently, library administrators who understand the tumult change causes, and who are somewhat prepared to cope with the amazing speed at which technological and social change impacts information patterns are in a unique position. They are the individuals most able to create a vision of the library future and to create alternate paths to it. They are the individuals most able to come to successful personal accommodation with the rate of exploding change. They are most able to effect substantive change in the library field. And, they are most suited to serve as its leadership, redirecting our library mission to better meet changing user needs.

MEGATRENDS

Megatrends are defined by Naisbitt as "broad outlines that will define a new society" (Naisbitt, 1982). His description synthesizes major United States trends at this time of technological and social transition and change. He identified these trends from content analysis of two million articles from local newspapers monitored over a twelve year period. Naisbitt's premise is that American trends move from the bottom up, fads move from the top down. Consequently, examining local news coverage of events and activities produces a relatively accurate identification of trends. From this analysis, he "outlines one interpretation of that future in order to make it more real, more knowable" (Naisbitt, 1982).

The credibility of these major trends Naisbitt has identified can be seen in the attention they have received from today's leaders in business organizations, in current management literature and in the warm reception given speeches, workshops and consultations offered by the Naisbitt Group. Therefore, it hardly seems presumptuous at this point to propose that they also carry significant implications for library leaders responsible to develop assumptions and plans that guide the library future.

Naisbitt identifies and describes ten key trends he finds destined to shape our future. Knowing them is the first step to developing creative and constructive responses.

1. *We have changed from an industrial society to an economy based on the creation and distribution of information.* The turning point into the post-industrial society was 1956-57 when information began to become the country's most important strategic resource. This fundamental change has caused significant shifts in the society, including automation and structural unemployment. The information based society is an economic reality and a technological possibility with the United States economy now based on the creation and distribution of information.

2. *For new technology applications introduced, compensatory human responses are required to assure acceptance of the technology.* People need balance. We seek to offset the dominance of "high tech," intense technology, that surrounds us and seek "high touch," greater human interaction.

3. *We are shifting from a national economy characterized by isolation and self sufficiency to being part of an interdependent global economy.* Our national economy is making major moves in the direction of an interdependent global and regional economy, yielding its position as the world's dominant economic force and becoming, instead, a member of the group of economically strong countries.

4. *We are moving from short-term considerations and rewards to favor much longer term time frames.* Our previous preoccupation with short term results and quantitative performance measurements have led to neglect of long range investments and innovations in business and organizations. Tomorrow's world, requires

strategic long range vision. We must rethink our basic goals in that light.

5. *We are shifting from centralized structures to decentralized ones.* Evident in political, economic, and business areas particularly, this change affirms the norm of greater involvement of diverse people and groups. According to Naisbitt, this, as a standard, can yield a more balanced and empowered society. Decentralization will be the primary mode ". . .to tackle problems and create change at local level."

6. *We seek greater self-reliance in all aspects of our lives.* This trend is seen in health care, home education, self-employment and food production and distribution. We are moving away from the patriarchal organization (e.g., government, institutions) as our employer or server. We more often seek freedom from conforming institutional structures preferring self-reliance and relearning to take action for self-help.

7. *The ethic of participation is widespread, altering the way we think people must be governed.* General acceptance is now given the precept that "people whose lives are affected by a decision must be part of the process of arriving at that decision." For example, corporate structures are being adapted to permit workers, shareholders, consumers, and community leaders a larger say in influencing how they are run. This ethic will eventually restructure all American institutions that serve and employ people.

8. *We are waiving our dependence on hierarchical structures in favor of informal networks.* Networks are "people talking to each other, sharing ideas, information, and resources." "Although sharing information and contacts is their main purpose, networks can go beyond the mere transfer of data to the creation and exchange of knowledge." They cut diagonally across organizations and attempt to connect people directly with the person or resource sought. Future organizational structures will be established and managed on this model with its values and its communication patterns rooted in informality and equality. This trend, evolving now, can be seen in such examples as Type Z organizations and the application of the quality circles concept.

9. *Power and population centers are shifting from the North and East to the Sunbelt and Florida.* This not only signifies demographics but patterns of lifestyle and work.

10. *We are increasingly becoming aware of multiple options, moving beyond operating as a narrow, forced choice society.* This "richness" in creating options and then making choices poses decision-making challenges, for individuals and organizations, that demand capabilities previously unknown.

These megatrend changes offer both rubric and context for library planners to address the library's position. The manager's planning function, critical in times of change, requires understanding these megatrends as the foundation for sound planning. Each megatrend must be weighed to discover its strength relevant to libraries. The library manager's strategic planning then plots change, anticipates breakthroughs and barriers, explores alternatives that will enhance the library's future ability to respond flexibly. With such vision and planning library decision-makers can create a viable, significant library future.

MARKETING LIBRARIES

Marketing is a vital element in the manager's planning function and in creating the future. Its role, when employed optimally, persists before, throughout and following planned change. Marketing is a planning tool that helps shape the vision, tests its feasibility, initiates and then modifies its operation. When done consciously and with skill, library marketing can maintain a visible, relevant library position.

Further, marketing is a managerial activity that helps decision-makers better understand, monitor and shape change. Managers aware of and skilled with marketing tools and concepts, ideally at least, are better able to anticipate and respond to megatrends. Marketing, as a concept and as a practice, still seems alien to many library managers, however. Until recently, little on marketing has appeared in library literature. Academic preparation for most present-day library managers did not include formal marketing exposure. As one consequence, marketing has been neither the accepted attitude nor common frame of reference in most library workplaces. One interpretation of this is that the marketing discipline, as such, may not be viewed as a legitimate library function.

Although often not done consciously or capably, marketing is not unknown in libraries. For example, when planning new facilities or services, library managers have consistently taken into account demographic shifts, patterns of use, user need and promotion efforts. Without the concept and consciousness of marketing per se, libraries nonetheless have found various pieces of the marketing function so essential that they have used them. Most often, however, marketing is equated with the discrete, traditional, and accepted practices such as publicity, public relations, bulletin boards and community outreach.

Kotler's (1975) definition of the marketing function best reveals its holistic nature and broad scope. He defines marketing as the organization's effective management of its exchange relations with its various publics. As such, it addresses the elements of intentional change, both internally (i.e., management) and externally (i.e., public). Marketing, particularly in its broad sense, opens greater capability for library adaptation and change.

Marketing begins with defining principle "markets" (i.e., users) both present and potential. This requires market (i.e., needs) analysis with consideration of the competition, the environment strengths and weaknesses within the constraint of the funding base and other factors. Next, how best to serve these markets is weighed to determine what products, services, materials are required. Then, alternative strategies that can produce and deliver these goods and services are developed. Finally, action plans map the best way to implement the decisions and monitoring/evaluation procedures are put in place. Essentially, marketing is the means used to examine and understand the present in terms of the user, and helps prepare for the future.

The strategic importance and contribution of the marketing function is becoming more evident. Significantly, pressures from all sides now urge library marketing efforts from a broader viewpoint. These pressures include greater managerial sophistication, education and training, contributions in library literature, and a heightened sense of need. Added to these pressures now come those from the megatrends themselves, addressing as several do, the core of the library mission.

Obviously, the trend Naisbitt lists first, the shift from an industrial to informational society, has great, direct and obvious implications for libraries. Yet, in spite of their strong emphasis on the vital nature of information in our world, the Naisbitt and Toffler titles ignore the present and future significance of libraries. Although Naisbitt quotes a Department of Commerce study that lists librarians as being a "primary information sector," he neither expands on this nor comments on the role or impact of libraries or librarians in relation to any of the megatrends described. Why is this? The lack of mention may be as important to us as any of the trends themselves. Both short and long range planning for the library future will need to take into account the "invisibility" of libraries, whether so perceived through oversight or intent.

The most pervasive and fundamental pressure from any of the megatrends, of course, is the shift from an industrial to an information age. Traditionally libraries have been centers providing organization and accessibility of written information. Now, business organizations, seeing the trend, engage in and market themselves as being in "the information business." They study information user groups targeting their marketing message(s) accordingly. Implications for libraries are direct and unequivocal. Unless the library message is clear, unless the library can deliver what it claims, it will be bypassed in favor of others that can do so. Libraries now face competition, stiff competition with management and marketing experience. Only the library that knows, articulates and fulfills a clear purpose will be perceived as a viable information organization. This calls for clear internal definition of purpose together with sound external marketing.

The challenge to set our purpose and develop our marketing strategies is dramatic and deserves concern. Seeing this challenge, forecaster F. Wilfrid Lancaster (1982) predicts "that electronic communication will continue to substitute for other forms, that electronic publishing will largely replace print-on-paper publishing, and that libraries as we now know them will become obsolete. The only uncertainty relates to the pace of change: How much will have occurred by when?"

He describes the library as a viable provider giving access to information and materials, a particularly valuable role during the transition period, (perhaps 20 years) but continuing after that only if it can adapt to a radically changing communication environment. "The survival of the library profession depends on its ability and willingness to change its emphasis and image" (Lancaster, 1982). In addition, he stresses, the profession must shift from its dependence on the library as a facility rather than on the technical expertise of its practitioners.

Lancaster's librarians may not be an endangered species, however. Contrary to his dour forecast about libraries, he sees the role of "professional information specialists" as invaluable in an electronic age. Although he does not indicate so specifically, marketing offers the possibility of changing the librarian's image and emphasis, offering them the capability to develop a purposive role for the transition and beyond. Certainly, marketing within the library field is as significant (an essential) as that done externally. To imagine "librarians" working without their usual institutional base and in the milieu of electronic publishing and communication stretches our traditional thinking.

The new visions generated by the ten megatrends raises some of the basic questions librarianship faces. The most basic one for us rises primarily from the first megatrend: what business are we really in? Naisbitt illustrates how vital this question is by relating the case of U.S. railroads. They viewed themselves in the railroad rather than the transportation business. The consequences of this narrow and rigid perspective and marketing approach are obvious. Some might perceive libraries as currently in painfully parallel circumstances. Relating the purpose of the library with its physical structure rather than its function has yielded short range vision and narrow parameters.

The library mission is also confronted by technology. Again, technology is widely adopted by non-library organizations engaging in "the information business." Naisbitt offers a helpful construct. He describes three stages of technological development. At first, new technology follows the line of least resistance and tends to be applied where relatively low opposition or high acceptance exists. In the second stage, new technology is introduced to improve previous technologies increasing their capability (such as speed or capacity) but not replacing their existing functions or purpose. Finally, in the third stage, new directions or functions emerge from applying new technologies. Naisbitt perceives most of our society in the second stage.

Many libraries adamantly resist automation. Those that have incorporated automated technologies have done so mostly to perform existing functions better but with little basic readjustment of the original purpose. A few, however, are in the initial stages of envisioning new purposes, experimenting with innovative functions and new technology. Often, implementation is doubtful. Certainly we continue to struggle with the impact of the information age and the new ideas it raises. Often, it appears difficult to give ready acceptance or even acknowledgement to new ideas (even those proffered from within the field) that might move more libraries beyond stage one and into stage two, then three. Currently, lively professional debate centers around the need for changed practices, image and functions. But, we need to move beyond this and act.

MEGATREND MARKETING

As the increasing impact of new technology and megatrends intensifies the pressure for change in libraries, the times call for long range, strategic planning and, as a significant component of that, clever marketing. Megatrends themselves, once identified and understood, can serve as a basis for tentative assumptions for managers who can then set directions for planned organizational change, incorporation of new technology and new community connections. They can also lead to creative library marketing efforts. Those described here are initial ideas of potential marketing efforts stimulated by reading and thinking about megatrends in relation to libraries.

Given the diverse possibilities offered by the megatrends that indicate decentralization will increase and the use of multiple options will proliferate, libraries will find their communities populated with decentralized structures, each having needs for information and the ability to share, coordinate and integrate it. Likewise, decentralization of the library, with corresponding local control, will surface greater citizen interest and involvement in what and how the library is doing. Libraries will find an even greater range demanded for their own different-ness as citizens demand unique adaptations of it to the local context. As libraries adapt, becoming more diverse in their structure, roles and functions, national standardization trends and funding sources may cease.

This picture of the possible even though only briefly described here indicates how deep the changes and how rich the marketing implications can be from exploring megatrends. The "exchange relations" with the library's public will be intricate, made complex by its own active governing bodies and more demanding users. The primarily local funding base will require viable local connections, especially political ones. The emphasis the past few years on community analysis and participative planning will be particularly suitable, basic even, for developing a sound marketing approach. These processes identify users' needs, carve out the library's distinct role and relationship with its community and guide the development of its services and products. They will also be invaluable to build two-way communication channels with the community that connect its diverse elements.

In such circumstances, a library's marketing effort might well capitalize on its information handling ability to assist community organizations to plan and deal capably with their information resources and needs. A role that might emerge for the library in this situation could be that of central community information clearinghouse. (Given the discomfort evidenced by many libraries with community information and referral as a library function, we can imagine the ease of this transition for administrators and personnel.) Building and maintaining the needed connections to sustain a sound political capability (and funding justification) will likely require extensive and continuous interpersonal dialogue between library personnel at various levels and the public.

Marketing thus will require internal consistency, personal conviction and a clear message to deliver at the same time as the community's multiple messages are being elicited, analyzed and channeled into library decisions. Library managers faced with necessary internal change and external shifts face challenges and an exciting new level of involvement. Managers and personnel alike will require communication skills, a high tolerance for ambiguity and the skill of effectively guiding processes through which participative decisions are made.

Another megatrend indicates that a "high tech, high touch" society will seek balance between technology and human interaction. Examining the lessons U.S. banks discovered when their move into electronic bank services brought a backlash of user resentment and employee sabotage, library planners can strive to assure that both technological capabilities and human interaction are elements of services. And, they can plan for appropriate communication capabilities linking these elements.

Because of its past heritage, the library may well be looked to as a "megatrend bridge" for many users. As they seek to adjust their lifestyles and job skills to new technologies, adults predictably will seek diverse ways to learn new skills for a changed world. They may seek a human source that can provide interpersonal contact to help them deal with the increasingly computerized system of information transfer.

Such new services as well as library technologies will need to be "user friendly" enabling users to identify and create their own options, then pursue their diverse goals. The image and ability of the library must be skillfully marketed to guide people to use its resources. For example, libraries might be marketed as a place to search, reflect and be with people for idea, social or work information exchange. Or, libraries may be marketed as the information source with a human touch.

Such a library requires personnel with a new level of skills, both technical and human. The ''megatrend bridge'' idea may be as needed inside the library as outside since library personnel face changes as startling as other community citizens. With effective marketing of a fresh library image new people and attitudes will be attracted to work in libraries. As employees, they too will seek suitable technology/human interaction balances in the positions they hold, in the careers they seek. Likely, too they will expect to participate actively within the library, bringing a wealth of diversity and expression that will, in turn, increase pressure for internal changes. They will seek openings for their creativity, job satisfaction and assertiveness. Marketing the library as a humane and yet technologically capable workplace will draw vital and different individuals to contribute to library change processes.

The megatrends revealing the ethic of participation in governance and that of seeking greater self-reliance surely speak to libraries. Libraries can well serve as great resources for the empowerment of the citizenry, both individually and collectively. More actively involved people feeling a sense of ownership, a natural inclination to be involved and a bent for self-reliance need many facts, opinions and sources. Marketing the library picture in response to this would be not unlike that of today except for depth and scope. ''Information professionals'' will be expected to take a more active role than now to acquire, interpret and connect users with information from people, print and electronic sources. Marketing this new scope inside and outside the library will require expanding the present image and developing new personnel capabilities to meet the new image. The marketing message could well be that the library enables individuals and the community as a whole to achieve a quality existence.

And finally, the megatrend that indicates a preference for network structures over hierarchical ones seems a natural for libraries since networks rely heavily on the acquisition and dissemination of information. Nonetheless, the development of people networks in the library field is much less advanced than that of hardware networks (i.e., utilities). Naisbitt refers to the former rather than the latter even though they may work at times in concert. Consequently, re-education in the field will be needed to become knowledgeable in ways to work together in network structures such as citizen's information groups where the need to acquire and exchange information will be intense. Libraries might well take the role of facilitating network initiatives and connections through active network brokering or by providing communication facilities that offer new ways for people to connect and collaborate on mutual interests. With capable marketing, libraries could be perceived as a unique and essential community function, an institution valued for how it enables individuals to connect through networks.

These are but some of the megatrend marketing possibilities that arise from musing about the future of libraries. At this point in our history, speculation about the future is an essential task, not a leisure-time activity—not only for library managers. As we view the marketing of libraries for a megatrend world, we are drawn to deeper exploration of our mission now and in the future. Grasping the scope and rapidity of the changes afoot is difficult. But sound planning and creative marketing of libraries is the only hope for their future.

CONCLUSIONS

Libraries are not adapting rapidly or substantively enough to respond to megatrend challenges. We must consider bold, fresh responses that respond to, or better, anticipate megatrend movements. With adaptation, libraries could be relevant in the new age. Redefined roles, relevant functions, innovative attitudes might assure libraries a place in the mainstream market. To be forerunners in the information business, libraries must meet their intensifying competition in sophistication and clarity and timeliness. The times are changing rapidly; libraries must change.

Megatrends will alter our personal as well as our work lives. Even though people and organizations are not easily changed, the transformation must come from within libraries and librarians as well as within the society. As we change libraries to meet the challenge of megatrends, we, ourselves will be transformed. Consequently, library administrators have a single responsibility. They are in a position to plan and direct organizational change and environments that foster personal adaptation.

Awareness of megatrends will aid library managers to envision the library's future. These visions construct a base for strategic planning designed to bring the library into that future. Planning and marketing must be geared to the library's unique qualities of broad access and balance in light of environmental and societal changes. Innovative efforts must modify traditional activities that are still viable for the new age. A broad marketing approach can help develop change strategies that prepare for a megatrend future.

Planning, with a strong marketing component, can analyze library functions, users and human resources, then determine how best to deliver services to those who need them in an acceptable and appropriate way. Planning efforts of managers, however, are only effective if a marketing attitude pervades the organization, implementing in the performance of everyday tasks. Marketing, thus, will serve as a path preparing libraries, librarians and our environment for different roles and functions. Planning and marketing are tools library managers must use to maintain diverse options and strengthen their future possibilities as well as maintain the present position for libraries to meet changing needs. Megatrends suggests those changing needs.

REFERENCES

Note: Reference for Schaar quote was used as a quote in: Hanberry, Gerald C. *Inventing the Future; Participatory Planning Process for Alternative Futures.* College Park, Md., University of Maryland University College, 1975. p. 12.

Toffler, Alvin. *Future Shock.* New York, Random House, 1970.

Toffler, Alvin. *Third Wave.* New York, Morrow, 1980.

Naisbitt, John. *Megatrends; Ten New Directions Transforming Our Lives.* New York, Warner Books, 1982.

Ibid. p. 2.

Ibid. p. 249.

Kotler, Philip. *Marketing for Nonprofit Organizations,* Englewood Cliffs, NJ., Prentice-Hall, 1975. p. x.

Lancaster, F. W. *Libraries and Librarians in an Age of Electronics,* Arlington, VA, Information Resources Press, 1982 p. 151.

Ibid. p. 169-170.

Naisbitt, *loc. cit.* p. 27.

Library Market Segmentation:
An Effective Approach
for Meeting Client Needs

Anne J. Matthews, M.A., Ph.D.

During the past five years library managers in all types of libraries have become increasingly aware of the possibilities and advantages of applying marketing concepts and strategies to the operation of their libraries. Library schools and associations have presented marketing institutes and seminars, articles and editorials have appeared in various professional journals, one School of Library and Information Management offers a full quarter course entitled, ''Marketing Library Services,'' and, in the best of library tradition, exhaustive bibliographies have been developed.

For the most part, these courses and articles have been addressed to all librarians and information workers in all types and sizes of libraries: an audience which in marketing terminology would be described as ''undifferentiated.'' Unfortunately, this is not too different from the approach taken by most libraries in offering their products and services to ''The Public'': an audience or market which consists of everyone in the community or university or company. Library market segmentation offers an approach to identifying and more effectively serving present and prospective publics.

MARKET SEGMENTATION

The process of Market Segmentation is fundamental to the whole idea of marketing, since it focuses on the customer, in this case the library's present or prospective user, rather than the product—the library's ''well balanced collection.'' A market segment may be defined as a group of customers with similar or related characteristics, who have common needs and wants, who will respond to like motivations, and who can be

---

Dr. Matthews is an Associate Professor, Graduate School of Librarianship and Information Management, University of Denver. She teaches courses in Marketing and Public Relations.

expected to use a service that fulfills these needs.[1] Too often librarians think in terms of what they feel the customer needs and wants, rather than identifying user groups, and tailoring the collection to their interests and desires. Library market segmentation takes into account the fact that library users who request a product or a service are all individuals who are unique in some way. Despite the claim of public libraries that they serve the "general public," few if any really do. In actuality they serve a series of market segments such as: preschool children; young adults; decision-makers; white middle class homemakers; elderly men and women who live in low income housing close to a downtown library, etc. Academic libraries propose to serve everyone in the university. They really serve segments of the academic community: research professors in chemistry; faculty who want leisure reading; information brokers who use the index/abstracting services, etc. No library or any other agency can reach all members of the community. Therefore it is essential that libraries, like other non-profit and for-profit organizations identify those parts of the mass market which they can most effectively serve. A first step in this process is to consider current users—those who have library cards, and who belong to segments such as those suggested above. Figures 1-4 illustrate the principle of identifying target market segments.

UNDIFFERENTIATED MARKETING

Traditionally, libraries have practiced mass marketing or undifferentiated marketing. By definition this means that the organization goes after the whole market with one offering, trying to attract as many consumers as possible,[2] attempting to be all things to all people. It treats all customers as similar, offers a standard product for everyone, and attempts to appeal to every eligible person to use its products (books, records, newspapers, data bases) and its services (reference help, story hours, cataloging). The assumption underlying undifferentiated marketing is that all people have similar or identical needs and it is important to focus on what is common to everyone, rather than on what is different. The rationale is that it is essential to appeal to the broadest number of users since all tax-payers underwrite the cost of a school or public or state-owned university library, and all must be served. Obviously there is some merit to this argument; however, research indicates that libraries are not now serving their largest potential market, and user satisfaction is diminished through the failure of the library to meet their varying and individual needs. The aggregate of all of the individuals and groups in Figures 1-4 represent the undifferentiated or mass market of each of the types of libraries. Market Segmentation divides the aggregate or mass market into smaller groups. A library which has a goal or mission state-

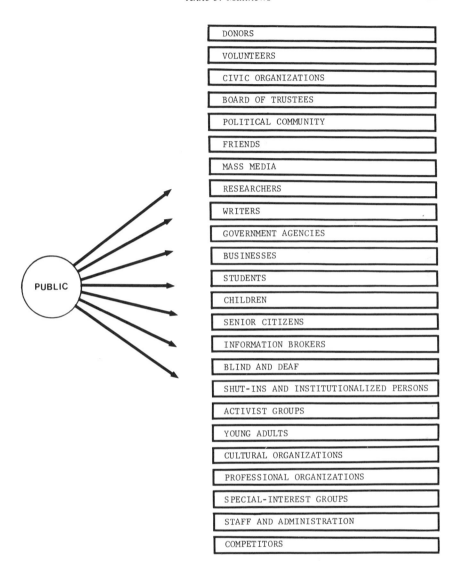

DONORS

VOLUNTEERS

CIVIC ORGANIZATIONS

BOARD OF TRUSTEES

POLITICAL COMMUNITY

FRIENDS

MASS MEDIA

RESEARCHERS

WRITERS

GOVERNMENT AGENCIES

BUSINESSES

STUDENTS

CHILDREN

SENIOR CITIZENS

INFORMATION BROKERS

BLIND AND DEAF

SHUT-INS AND INSTITUTIONALIZED PERSONS

ACTIVIST GROUPS

YOUNG ADULTS

CULTURAL ORGANIZATIONS

PROFESSIONAL ORGANIZATIONS

SPECIAL-INTEREST GROUPS

STAFF AND ADMINISTRATION

COMPETITORS

FIGURE 1

ment declaring that its purpose is to meet ''The educational, recreational and informational needs of the total community (or university) by providing a well balanced collection of materials'' needs to consider one of the following strategies.

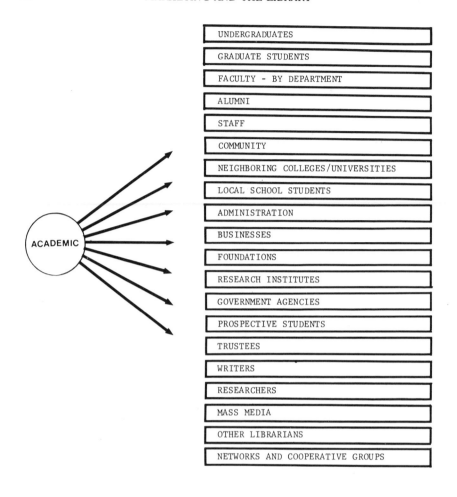

FIGURE 2

CONCENTRATED MARKETING

While libraries which practice undifferentiated marketing attempt to meet the needs of the entire population and treat all present and potential users as similar, offering a standard collection for everyone, concentrated marketing goes to the opposite extreme and attempts to concentrate all of its efforts on one specific segment, serving that group particularly well. If this strategy were carried to its ultimate conclusion, each individual user could be thought of as a potentially separate market segment, arguing that the needs, interests, attitudes and behavior patterns of each person are slightly different from everybody else, and it is necessary to customize services and select materials to meet the needs of each individual. Obviously there are limits as to how far concentrated marketing can be car-

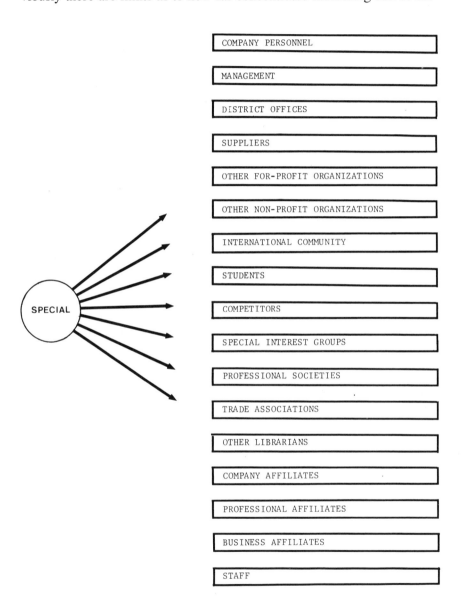

FIGURE 3

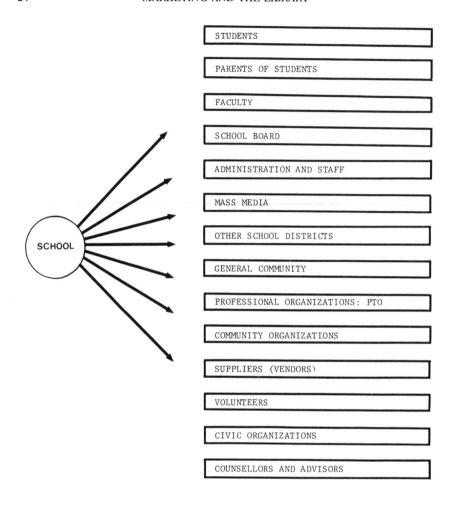

FIGURE 4

ried. The famous injunction to provide "The right book to the right person at the right time" could be considered an application of concentrated marketing. This type of marketing is done by special libraries which serve very homogeneous users and concentrate on a particular market segment. Special libraries' staff must know the needs and wants of their specific audience, must analyze their behavior patterns, and select and provide materials and services based on the needs of that one group. Thus, while concentrated marketing would not be cost effective for a metropolitan public library, it provides an economical advantage to an industrial research library which needs fast and accurate information in order to keep ahead in a competitive field.

DIFFERENTIATED MARKETING

Differentiated Marketing is the term used when an organization has divided the mass market into smaller groups (Figures 1-4), and decides to go after two or more market segments by developing an effective service or product for each of the chosen segments. This concept groups consumers into segments on the basis of intra-group similarities and inter-group differences, as shown in Figures 1-4.[3] Differentiated marketing strategy recognizes the varying needs of the users, and provides a rationale for examining individuals and groups who are non-users. By dividing the entire population into target groups, it is possible to notice market segments whose needs are not currently being met. As the library manager looks at specific groups, he or she is better able to identify their special needs, interview members of the group to learn what they want, develop plans to meet expressed needs, and attempt to influence group members to use the library's resources. This marketing strategy follows the following steps:

1. Classify the present and potential users by their basic needs and wants. (A need is something one ought to have and a want is something one would like to have.)
2. Identify what benefits the members of the group are seeking. (Economic—saves cost of buying the books; time—can look something up quickly.)
3. Consider the significant characteristics of each target market (age, lifestyle, location, education). Also include size of the target group, where located, and who your competition may be. (Bookstores, other libraries.)
4. Isolate environmental influences which impact the group, such as economic, political, social or other factors.
5. Decide on the number of target groups which the library can feasibly serve or attract, and define and describe each market segment which is selected.

Several criteria must be applied in the process of selecting target groups. These include:

1. *Accessibility:* Can the segment be reached in a cost-effective way?
2. *The focus of the group:* Is there a commonality of interests, shared needs, wants and preferences?

3. *Viability:* Is the size and composition of the group large enough to merit special planning?
4. *Opportunity to the library* to create new programs, plan new services and eliminate obsolete offerings.
5. *Staff considerations:* Better utilization of specialists, and the opportunity to encourage creativity.
6. *Relation to other market groups:* Is this a distinct group or does it overlap or conflict with other groups?
7. *Timing:* Can the library meet the needs of this group in a reasonable period of time, or anticipate its future needs?
8. *Public Relations emphasis:* Does this group provide an improved focus for planning appropriate services which can be promoted to the advantage of the library?
9. *Loyalty:* Is this a group which can be encouraged to continue to use the services and products of the library?
10. *Alternatives:* What is the advantage of choosing this group over any or all of the others under consideration?[4]

Once the target groups have been selected, using these or similar criteria, the library must design and/or tailor products and services to meet the needs of the group, establish pricing (how much will it cost the library and the customer to provide these services), and decide how best to communicate or publicize the program.

MARKET SEGMENTATION IN DEPTH

Each of the target markets identified in Figures 1-4 can further be segmented in order to more effectively serve the individuals within any given group. Kotler states that there is no one, or right way to segment a market; (a market being defined as the set of actual and potential customers for your products, programs and services.) A market can be segmented in a number of ways by introducing different variables and seeing which reveal the most in the way of market opportunities.[5] For example, in Figure 1, consider the target group, "Senior Citizens." The public library which chooses this group as one of its primary targets may do so for one or more of the following reasons:

1. A retirement community is being planned within walking distance of the library (geographical segmentation).
2. The most recent census reports that the average age of the population within a one-mile radius of the library is over 55 years of age (demographic segmentation).
3. A community life-style study reveals that the elderly have above

average incomes and frequently visit museums and attend lectures (psychographic segmentation).
4. An in-house survey shows a 10% increase in six months in the number of people over 60 years of age who are using the library—indicating a growing and increasingly loyal user group (behavioristic segmentation).

Any or all of the above data may be sufficient to convince a library administrator or planner that Senior Citizens comprise a meaningful target group. It is now time for an in-depth analysis in order to learn as much as possible about this particular market segment. Several key questions must be answered:

1. Who are the potential users in this market?
2. What are their library needs?
3. Do they recognize their needs?
4. Which of their needs are we serving now?
5. What benefits do they receive?
6. Where are they located?
7. Are they physically able to use the library?
8. What services are appropriate for us to offer this group?
9. How can we reach them with our message?
10. What is the exchange potential in impacting this group?
11. What are their attitudes toward the library?

The tools of marketing research will assist the librarian in finding answers to these questions. Some useful approaches include face-to-face and telephone interviews, a check of registration files, questionnaires, in-house surveys, and observation of current use patterns.

Segmentation Variables

The four major variables referred to earlier are widely used by marketers to gain insights into the market.

Demographic Segmentation, such as age, sex, income, occupation, education, religion, race and nationality, are popular ways to look at consumer groups. "Senior Citizens" are, by current definition, all people who are over 55 years of age. Obviously, this is too broad a definition to be meaningful, and it may be necessary to categorize the elderly more closely: under 70 (the young old) and over 70 (the old old). Even this further refinement leaves us with a number of questions: Are they active or inactive? Healthy or ailing? Other demographics of importance to libraries have to do with *education:* What types of materials should be available; with *income:* Do they buy their own books or prefer to borrow them; with *occupation:* Are they retired, or working full or part-time? What is their present or past occupation? *Sex:* Are they male or female? Geriatric research indicates that in the over-65 population, women outnumber men: Is this true in your group? Were the women homemakers or did they work outside the home before their retirement?

Geographical Segmentation: Where do the Senior Citizens live? Are they living in their own homes? Apartments? Low income housing? Some retirement communities require a substantial entrance fee, as well as a monthly stipend. This may be an indicator of the affluence—and homogeneity—of the elderly who live in a particular complex. Likewise there may be a religious or ethnic interest which attracts the elderly to a certain neighborhood or geographic area. Is there a move to—or away—from the city? Have they recently moved to a different part of the country?

Psychographic Segmentation[6] examines attitudes, living styles, personality, and social classes. Senior Citizens may have a past history of using libraries, and have a positive attitude toward them, but need to be reminded of their services. If the seniors have outgoing, gregarious personalities, they could be considered potential volunteers. They may be experimenting with new life styles (living together to avoid paying higher taxes). Many Senior Citizens are in new environments, lonely, and could be encouraged to become involved.

Behavioristic Segmentation.[7] By examining usage behavior, libraries can identify users, non-users, ex-users and first-time users. The library can appeal to Senior Citizens on the basis of offering excellent service and programs which are relevant and useful to them. They may be particularly interested in leisure-time activities, prefer fiction to non-fiction, and want to read things which previously they haven't had time to read. Library programs could explore timely subjects such as nutrition, exercise, saving money, health concerns and tax advice. In terms of "buyer readiness," the elderly are probably more ready to use library services than ever before: They have the time to develop new interests, have the need for certain types of specialized material (large print books, audiotapes), and have the background and experience to make a contribution to the library. Exchange is the basis of marketing: Senior citizens can give time to the library as volunteers, take books to the homebound and work on book sales in exchange for using the materials and services of the library.

PRODUCT/MARKET SEGMENTATION

In addition to the variables which concentrate on the user, libraries can segment their market by concentrating on their products. Consider the following questions:

1. Do the current products, programs and services meet the needs of the target groups which the library wishes to impact?
2. Will it be necessary to develop new products in order to reach a new market segment?
3. Are there competitors who have similar products, such as other libraries, bookstores, museums? Why should this target group use your library?
4. Are there programs or books which should be eliminated? Remember the adage that circulation usually goes up after a collection has been weeded.
5. Can your products—books, magazines, art prints—be displayed more attractively?
6. If there is a Com Cat or an on-line catalog, is it clearly visible? Are there step-by-step instructions, with illustrations, for using it?
7. Does the reference collection reflect the needs of the current users or is it based on an "average standard collection"?

A product/market segmentation grid may assist decision makers to think insightfully across a set of variables as they carry out market planning for their libraries. For example, an academic library administrator and planning officer examine the various present or potential target audiences of the library and agree that the primary market segment is the faculty. The next most meaningful group is the entire student body, both undergraduates and graduates. They are aware that the university has recently conducted a study of enrollment trends which indicates that there has been an increase in the number of graduate students entering the university during the past two years. The library planning team decides that this is a distinct target group which merits attention. They develop a product/market grid which includes the three target groups (current users), and several services which are presently offered (products 1-4, Figure 5). Product 5 is a service which will be added as an inducement to attract both faculty and graduate students to use the library's computer data bases.

The product/market segmentation grid is a tool which allows flexibility in decision-making, while forcing policy and decision makers to think specifically about which markets to penetrate. Academic libraries, by definition, must serve faculty, students, and administrators by providing books, journals, inter-library loan, reference services, etc. It is not possible to eliminate any of the primary market segments or basic products, but the grid provides a tool which the manager may use in year-by-year planning. While existing conditions dictate that some products and services apply to all target groups, it may be desirable to penetrate one cell and allocate extra budget in that area for one year. In the example above, the grid shows the planning team that as a group the faculty currently

FIGURE 5

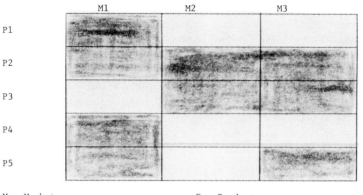

M = Market
M1 = Faculty
M2 = All Students
M3 = Graduate Students

P = Product
P1 = Unlimited borrowing privileges
P2 = Leisure reading
P3 = Bibliographic instruction
P4 = Preparation of Bibliographies
P5 = Computer database instruction

receives the most services. However, according to a recent user study, the team knows that faculty are not using the library very heavily.

The planners decide that the library must continue to give "bread and butter" service to all users, but it is important to concentrate on the faculty as a market segment, and to develop a marketing mix to more effectively meet their needs. The marketing mix includes one new *product* (in this example, computer base instruction); the *place* (put a computer terminal in each department so faculty can search the data bases without having to go to the library); *price* (estimate cost for this service and increase budget allocations); and *promotion* (let the faculty know what is being planned by mailing announcements to each person, telephoning key people to discuss the new product, putting posters in the faculty club and departmental offices, and alerting the entire library staff to the new service).

In this particular example, two market segments will benefit from the addition of one new product. While impacting the primary market—faculty—the library is also reaching an emerging market—graduate students.

A product/market grid gives a quick graphic overview of which products are being offered to which target groups. It helps planners in their decisions to add or eliminate services, to shift focus from one group to another, or to cut a notch or two deeper into one or more categories. Each of these decisions must, of course, be made in the light of the library's stated objectives and its financial resources.

Libraries are in the business of serving the people in their communities with products which meet their informational, educational, recreational and social needs and wants, as cost effectively as possible. Market segmentation provides the perspective and criteria to assist library managers to meet this challenge responsively and responsibly. It is not a panacea which will solve all problems, but it is an innovative approach to meeting the goal of responsive library service.

REFERENCES

1. Edward McKay, *The Marketing Mystique* (New York: American Management Association, 1972): 113.

2. Philip Kotler, *Marketing for Nonprofit Organizations,* 2nd edition (New York: Prentice-Hall, 1982): 228.

3. Christopher H. Lovelock, "A Market Segmentation Approach to Transit Planning, Modeling and Management," in *Marketing in Private and Public Nonprofit Organizations,* Ralph M. Gaedeke, ed. (Santa Monica: Goodyear Publishing Co., 1977): 127-128.

4. For a fuller discussion of this subject, see Edward McKay, *The Marketing Mystique,* Chapter 11: 103-120.

5. Philip Kotler, *Marketing for Nonprofit Organizations:* 219.

6. Other approaches to Psychographic Segmentation are discussed by Alan Andreasen in "Advancing Library Marketing," *Journal of Library Administration* (Fall, 1980): 17-32 and Morris Massey in "Market Analysis and Audience Research for Libraries," *Library Trends* 24 (January 1976): 473-481.

7. Philip Kotler, *Marketing for Nonprofit Organizations:* 219-224.

The ABCs of Implementing Library Marketing

Andrea C. Dragon, Ph.D.
Tony Leisner, M.B.A.

In his excellent review of the literature of marketing for libraries and information services, O. Gene Norman[1] quotes from Ralph M. Gaedeke, "no longer is the issue whether marketing concepts and techniques can be transferred to more effectively manage products and services of nonprofit organizations but, rather, the extent, nature, and effectiveness of such transfer."[2] Indeed, the missionary zeal with which articles on marketing are written[3] is indicative of a wide-spread grassroots movement within the profession. This interest in marketing is not the result of a mandate from the leaders of the professional associations nor is it due to any governmental action. This "bottom-up" interest in marketing has grown out of librarians desire to find a more appropriate model for relating their professional activities to their community's needs.

The fact that the library profession has begun to take a keen interest in learning about marketing does not mean that it is universally accepted as an appropriate model for the conduct of library business. Barbara Conroy[4] has written that she believes much of the reluctance to practice marketing in a public service setting is due to a misunderstanding of marketing and its relationship to public service programming. Conroy believes that once librarians understand that marketing and library programs are really quite similar, the hesitancy will diminish.

Another writer voicing criticism of the marketing model is John Dessauer.[5] He states that his misgivings about library marketing stem from his firm belief that libraries are "depositories of civilization" and if a library builds a collection based upon user statistics, then it is not fulfilling its true mission.

John Berry[6] also questions the basic premise of whether libraries need to market themselves. Instead, he argues for libraries to continue to treat information as a "free" resource which should not be subjected to the laws of the marketplace.

Andrea C. Dragon is an Assistant Professor, School of Communication, Information and Library Studies, Rutgers, the State University of New Jersey. Tony Leisner is the Vice President of Quality Books, Northbrook, Illinois.

Both Dessauer and Berry miss the mark in their attempt to dissuade librarians from adopting marketing. Their arguments fail because they are over sentimentalized. Dessauer speaks of "an amateur scholar devouring volumes on ancient Egypt . . . a reader encountering Plato for the first time . . . the armchair mountain-climber, the sedentary sailor, the supine warrior."[7] Somehow, Dessauer is unable to connect these idyllic figures with the reality of the librarian who has determined the needs of the market and carefully selected material to satisfy those needs. The patrons using Dessauer's romanticized library are doing so because they have needs or problems that have been recognized by the library staff who then developed a product mix to satisfy those needs.

Understanding patron needs and designing products and services to meet those needs *is* marketing. The librarian who selects books about ancient Egypt for the armchair archaeologist is engaging in a marketing activity.

Dessauer questions a library buying materials readily found in bookstores and on newsstands. He would prefer that libraries serve those patrons whose needs cannot easily be met through these channels.

Critics of marketing would have us believe that offering patrons Louis L'Amour is "marketing" but offering them Plato and Voltaire is "professional collection development".

Although much of what Dessauer says is emotionally appealing, he forgets that for too long libraries have attempted to satisfy market segments whose needs closely parallel their own. While this type of marketing can be successful in communities where there are large segments of the population demographically similar to librarians, in other communities the social and demographic characteristics of the market require a different response from the local library.

While some libraries may believe their mission is to continue the tradition of "cultural uplift" associated with 19th century library associations, many other libraries believe their mission is to be responsive to the public needs even if those needs are not for the kind of information and reading material librarians think is appropriate.

Despite the growing interest and awareness of marketing, we believe that some librarians might continue to be less than enthusiastic about the implementation of marketing even if they were provided a thorough explanation of marketing essentials. They might be so included for very good reasons. The ideal of professional librarianship emphasizes the triple role of the librarian as an interpreter of information needs, as a communicator of knowledge about information resources and as a designer of information access systems. These roles are congruent with those described in a recent article on motivation and organizational design by John B. Miner and Norman R. Smith.[8] The authors outline five roles professionals assume in organizations and describe the motivational basis of each. The five roles are:

1. Acquiring further knowledge
2. Abiding by professional behavior standards
3. Accepting status
4. Providing assistance
5. Taking independent action

The authors state:

> In a professional system, the professional is expected to assist the client in achieving desired goals or, in some instances, to do that which is specified by the profession as being in the client's best interest, even if not consciously desired; to function effectively, a professional must want to help others.[9]

In other words, the professional must put his/her interests behind those of the client and society.

Because librarians have become so involved in the process of acquiring professional status by obtaining credentials, i.e., the M.L.S., most librarians use the term "professional" as a noun to describe someone who has obtained the M.L.S. and who has achieved a certain "rank" within the library organization enabling the individual to work somewhat independently and without close supervision.

The roles professionals aspire to and the motivational bases for them as described by Miner and Smith may conflict with a marketing orientation as defined by Philip Kotler,

> A marketing orientation holds that the main task of the organization is to determine the needs and wants of target markets and to satisfy them through the design, communication, pricing and delivery of appropriate and competitively viable products and services.[10]

If the term "professional" is used as an adjective it is almost always used to describe those tasks falling under the purview of the "professional librarian". For example, original cataloging is a "professional" activity but filing is not. Professional librarians, those who possess the M.L.S., carefully guard their rank and its privileges and often refuse to do "non-professional" tasks or allow "non-professionals" to work on professional ones.

Given this almost military concern with degrees, rank and credentials, it is no wonder that many librarians express confusion or perhaps even hostility when faced with the possibility of diminishing their status.

Contrasting with this marketing orientation is a professional (used as a librarian would use the term) orientation which holds that the major task of the organization is to develop programs and products which it believes are satisfying to the public and do not conflict with the professional role to which librarians aspire. In an organization dominated by such an orientation those products and services which enhance the professional's self-esteem will be preferred over those which do not. Any library manager contemplating implementing marketing must be prepared to debate with staff members who perceive marketing as a threat to their personal status. These staff members will question the necessity of acknowledging the primacy of the marketplace in shaping the library's plans, objectives, organizational design and day-to-day operations. To many librarians the term "professional" does not describe a way of behaving toward clients, but rather it connotes images of independence, self-direction, freedom from supervising controls and acknowledgement from non-professional library workers of acquired status. The history of librarianship in America is a struggle to provide this sort of professional status for graduates of library schools. It is no wonder then that some librarians question the value of marketing which they perceive as perhaps reducing their status to that of a bookstore clerk. For while professionals generally perceive no conflict between their professionalism and promoting library products or encouraging library use, they hesitate to relinquish their role as arbiter in determining what those products will be and how access to them shall be gained. But, unless staff members recognize the importance of *designing the organization* to serve not the needs of the librarians but to serve the needs of chosen markets, the library is not engaging in marketing even though it may be actively promoting library use.

RESPONDING TO THE MARKET

Kotler maintains that organizations fail to be responsive, i.e., make every effort to sense, serve, and satisfy the needs and wants of their clients and publics within the constraints of budgets, for three reasons. The first reason offered by Kotler is that organizations may lack the resources or the power to hire, train, motivate and monitor the performance of employees. The second reason is that customer satisfaction may not be important to the members of the organization and its management. The third reason offered is that the organization may be deliberately acting in such a way as to discourage use by the public.

The conditions underlying Kotler's three reasons for unresponsiveness are found in varying degrees in all libraries. But, it is not possible to change libraries from their current varying states of unresponsiveness to being marketing-oriented, responsive organizations merely by educating management personnel in marketing fundamentals. Implementation of a marketing plan requires a commitment from every member of the library staff. If staff members are continually forced to choose between achieving professional and marketing objectives, they probably will choose the objectives whose accomplishment will lead to the greater personal rewards. Sitting passively at the reference desk waiting for someone to ask a question is very appealing to many librarians. Once a question is asked, they are comfortable only in seeking the appropriate information. But, if the management were to insist that reference librarians move away from the desk and initiate reference transactions with patrons, many staff members would find such behavior uncomfortable. It is not that management lacks the resources to hire, train, motivate and monitor the performance of employees that causes library failure to achieve a true marketing orientation. Rather, it is because library managers themselves are professionals who seek to hire and reward like-minded individuals. If library managers desire to change the behavior of their staff members, they must first change the way they reward staff behavior. If a library manager primarily uses technical competence as criteria for distributing organizational rewards, then staff members will strive to become competent, efficient, consistent and accurate. On the other hand, if managers begin to also recognize and reward those individuals who are willing to develop organizational systems that are accurate and responsive, consistent and compassionate, efficient and sensitive, then, librarians might be more inclined to behave in a market-oriented manner toward patrons. At the present time, most library operational systems are designed to meet the library's needs. New systems and individual capacities combining librarians' needs and public needs will have to be created before the library will become truly responsive.

In order to assist library managers in implementing marketing in their libraries, we suggest that directors keep in mind what we call the "ABCs of implementing marketing". These are:

— Achieving a Position
— Balancing Demands with Resources
— Compensating Performance

ACHIEVING A POSITION

The principle underlying positioning is the identification of the major attributes used by the target market to evaluate potential and choose among competitors. It is a process of understanding the needs of various target markets and of communicating to the targets the advantages of library use when compared to the alternatives for satisfying informational or recreational needs. Positioning is not just advertising or promotion, although advertising is often used to communicate a library's position, rather it refers to the perception of the library's placement within the array of competitors for the patron's and funding sources support.

One barrier to achieving any particular position is staff resistance. Someone hired to be a general reference librarian may balk at the prospect of becoming a readers' advisor should the library decide to assume a strong position in the family entertainment market. Someone with a background and expertise in the arts and humanities may resist efforts to reposition the library as a community information and referral center. Someone who has enjoyed cataloging science and technology may not approve of the library's decision to reduce emphasis in science and take a strong position in the business and economics information market. As regional and multitype library networks become more common, it is conceivable that public libraries will be making positioning decisions. The library that tries to be all things to all people will become less common as libraries begin to respond to the needs of their community by developing unique marketing positions tailored to the demographic characteristics and the unmet needs of the community. Achieving a position might make good marketing sense, but to some professionals working in the library, it is an objective that conflicts with what they understand about the library's mission and about their role as librarians.

Unlike businesses, libraries cannot easily terminate those who disagree with management's objectives. A manager who understands the necessity for a marketing orientation needs to be patient and understanding with staff members who remain unconvinced. Disagreements will be frequent and sometimes uncomfortable for all concerned. Achieving a position can be an exciting, satisfying and ego-boosting goal for the entire staff if it is presented as a method of responding to the community.

BALANCING DEMANDS WITH RESOURCES

The goal of any marketing effort is to change the behavior of the target market. In library marketing the change sought is usually increased use by the selected targets. In marketing-oriented libraries, more use is better than less. For the most part, the patron manifests satisfaction with the library by repeat use.

It is possible that successful marketing may increase utilization to the point where staff may become overwhelmed. The library traditionally placed limits or controls on market demand by enforcing silence rules, closing stacks, restricting hours, and fining. In addition to these methods, the library staff controlled demand through a system of subtle, and sometimes not so subtle, behaviors designed to communicate to the market that there were definite limits to how far the staff was willing to go to accommodate the patron. In profit making organizations, price acts as an effective control on demand, but in non-profit organizations, especially non-revenue organizations, demand cannot be controlled by price. Given the inability of libraries to quickly respond to increased demand by adding staff, staff behavior, policies and rules have been the only means available to the library to limit demand.

Library architecture and staff demeanor have changed in recent decades to create a library environment which is less imposing, less restrictive, and more accessible. Libraries have advocated the concept of free and unlimited service. The consequences of these changes include vagrants sleeping in urban public libraries, sexual deviants molesting patrons in the stacks, and teenagers monopolizing suburban reference rooms weekday evenings. It has been difficult for libraries to have an "open door" policy promising free and easy access and yet place restrictions on use by some segments.

In order to balance demands with available resources, libraries have instituted circulation restrictions, limited the number of reference questions per telephone inquiry and placed limits on "free" on-line searching. Other controls on library use include full-time security patrols and restricting teenage use.

Even with these balancing mechanisms, many librarians find that they are sometimes subjected to unreasonable service requests. Because the public in general is unsure to what level of service it is entitled, it is not uncommon for some members of the community to insist on service above and beyond that which the library feels is adequate. For these patrons, a policy promising free and unlimited service gives them the right to treat librarians as servants. Without the ability to demand money in exchange for service, the librarian must respond to the demand or establish rules (written or unwritten) governing the delivery of service.

Some librarians are fearful that increased marketing activity will have the desired effect of increasing library use, but increased use might also bring with it the potential for abuse. A librarian on the 6 to 10 p.m. shift with a library full of rowdy teenagers has good reason to be apprehensive about making the library more accessible and perhaps more vulnerable to certain market segments. Unless demand can be balanced with resources, the library's staff may become deluged with special requests and demands and be unable and/or unwilling to meet them.

There are several strategies available to libraries which help balance scarce resources with demands. The library will probably wish to avoid instituting rules and policies which will affect all segments and therefore might adversely impact the selected targets. Instead, a multi-branch library might consider branch specialization, i.e., The Children's Library, The Business and Economics Library, The General Literature Library, The Reference Library, etc.

Libraries unable to implement branch specialization may wish to prepare and publish service policies so that both librarian and patron will have a clearer understanding of the library's service limitations. This strategy has the advantage of being inexpensive yet it makes public the range of services patrons are entitled to receive given the library's limited resources. It seems important that there be a uniform service policy within a library. Each staff member ought to know what range of services will be offered and agree with the extent to which those services will be delivered to individual patrons.

COMPENSATING PERFORMANCE

One way to motivate librarians to substitute marketing objectives for technical ones is to reward them when they perform appropriately. Obviously, in some areas technical expertise is vital, but technical competencies ought to become less important to a marketing-oriented organization as an individual moves up in the administrative hierarchy. At some point the technical appropriateness of a serials entry ought to become less important than its ability to provide an access point for the patron.

Libraries have traditionally rewarded their staffs according to various professional criteria. Only rarely do these criteria include marketing-oriented behavior. Most of the time professionals are rated on subjective evaluations or attitudinal or personality traits.[11] If librarians include performance measures as part of their appraisal and compensation systems, they are usually no more than listings of routine tasks whose completion is perceived to be an objective. Most technical service librarians are able to produce a list of professionally satisfying objectives. But librarians should be encouraged to produce a list of objectives indicating a recognition of the importance of the market if a marketing plan is to become more than an academic exercise. Staff members should be rewarded if the objectives are accomplished.

Many library managers believe that bureaucratic rigidities, non-confidential payroll records, union contracts and civil service protections prevent the implementation of performance-based monetary reward systems. Unable to manipulate the monetary reward system, library managers reward performance by promotion into newly-created job classifications or creating changes in the organizational chart enabling highly performing staff members to enjoy a more favorable working climate.

The pitfall in using these kinds of administrative rewards is that because they lie outside the formal reward structure, the reasons for granting the reward to an individual may never be fully articulated. Unless the person receiving the promotion or title change understands the relationship between his or her performance and administrative outcomes, these kinds of non-monetary rewards may not provide a continuing source of motivation to engage in appropriate behavior. Performance that is seldom rewarded will become increasingly less important to most workers. But, if the link between performance and rewards is made clear to the staff and reinforced by management's actions, then staff performance ought to improve in the areas rewarded. Employees believing that rewards are distributed according to a system unrelated to performance will have a low expectation that their efforts and abilities will result in being rewarded and therefore have diminished interest in improving performance.

Because the traditional role of a professional librarian may be perceived as being in conflict with that of a marketing-oriented librarian, it is crucial to the success of a marketing plan to ensure compliance with marketing objectives. Excellent target market research, excellent audience-oriented program planning, excellent product design will all be costly, fruitless, wasted activities if the library staff cannot be convinced to behave toward the public in a manner consistent with a marketing orientation. Unless library managers inform librarians of behavior requirements they will substitute a variety of role models, many of which are not appropriate to a marketing-oriented library. Of course, managers could select only those who share the belief in the value of marketing. But, because only technical/professional competencies and not marketing ones are taught in most library schools, a library manager needs to recognize that he or she has the responsibility for training staff so that they will be able to engage in the appropriate behaviors. Finally, although selection and training are important determinants of performance, the most powerful performance determinant is the availability of rewards. By compensating those who behave in a marketing-oriented way, the library manager instructs the entire staff in appropriate behavior.

It is a great deal easier to write about marketing than to implement it in libraries. Despite the obvious advantages of a marketing orientation over a professional/product orientation, some librarians, in all likelihood, are apt to experience a role conflict between what they believe is appropriate professional conduct and the behavior requirements of a marketing-oriented organization. Rather than dismiss this role conflict as caused by some perversity in the librarian's personality, we have suggested that library administrators (some may even experience the role conflict themselves) implement library marketing by: achieving a position through a program of assisting the staff in learning about marketing and the need for positioning; balancing demand with available resources by developing service policies; compensate performance by rewarding marketing-oriented behavior.

CASE STUDIES

The following case studies are examples of public libraries which have been able to plan and implement successful marketing programs. These cases are supplied to demonstrate that the implementation of (A)— Achieving a position can be accomplished by vastly different methods in response to (B)—A need to balance demands with resources when demand is growing and resources are shrinking and that the answer need not be to reduce service; and (C)—That faced with probable cutbacks an inspired staff can help to not only avoid cutbacks, but obtain raises as a result of their enthusiasm for a bold move.

Janesville Public Library

Janesville, Wisconsin is a city that prides itself on government efficiency and at the end of 1981 was dealing with the annual budgets for city services. The city transit system got its budget cut by $150,000, the city landfill cut back by $80,000, and the garbage collection budget took a $30,000 beating. Building inspections were cut back in their hours saving $18,000 and even street sweeping was carved up.

In this budget slashing environment the Janesville Public Library budget was *increased* by 17.1%. One week later an agreement was reached finalizing a contract that made library director Dan Bradbury a dual administrator. His time would now be split between library functions and the duties of Director of Leisure Services which included recreational programs, golf courses, the senior citizens center, ball fields, the ice arena and swimming pool complex. Also included were the city's other cultural activities and some planning for a potential cultural center.

Discussions leading up to the contract had been going on since early June of 1981 with numerous city officials including the city manager, director of personnel and the city attorney. The agreed upon objective for both the city and Mr. Bradbury was to unify the city's informational, recreational and cultural services under one umbrella.

From a memo from Mr. Bradbury to the Board: "For the City, the new structure would unify the strategic planning and budgeting for facilities and services which currently dispersed among three different city divisions or departments. For the library the new structure would firmly identify the library as an integral component in the full range of municipal services while maintaining its autonomy of operation. In the long run the closer relationship with the city should facilitate the achievement of many of our library objectives—increased co-operation and coordination with Recreation Department Programming, improved communication and cooperation with all city departments, development of municipal reference and other services and participation in planning an eventual civic/cultural center complex."

One of the realities in government at almost any level today is that a tough general economic situation has had a severe impact on social services. At the same time that unemployment is rising, revenues are falling, government outflow increases and so called "free" services have more customers. Each of the social services has its own axe to grind and wants to protect its own vested interests and it is unlikely that a director of a department will volunteer to take a cut. This is particularly true when demand for the services is increasing. In the face of a 15-20% unemployment rate in Janesville, due in large part to its major employer being General Motors, it would be difficult for all public services to survive equally intact. Still the library got a 17.1% increase.

While no formal marketing plan existed at the Janesville Public Library a case could well be made that some basic marketing strategy was employed. In this declining economic setting the cultural, recreational and leisure activities providers have become competitors for limited resources no different than Coke, Pepsi and R.C. compete in the soft drink market. Just as no grocery store would remove Coke from the shelves in favor of Pepsi because of the public that wants Coke, neither will a city cut out a program with a voting block constituency that wants that service. The problem for the city government is how to measure the various services and the values placed on them by the public. Then funds must be allocated based on that assumption of value.

Janesville Public Library had already indicated its desire to reduce costs among agencies by offering to coordinate acquisitions, cataloging and processing of library materials for five other public libraries in the county and a dozen school media centers resulting in substantial savings to all agencies. Janesville Public Library also had begun a volunteer program which had contributed over 6500 hours of time to the library and had a 450 member Friends of the J.P.L. group. The Friends had raised over $17,000 for equipment purchases in about two years. In 1980 a foundation was established for the purpose of soliciting and administering grants, gifts and endowments to benefit library programs in Janesville and it has raised nearly $50,000.

The public library was clearly positioned as the low cost, efficient provider of services to a large portion of leisure activities users. Positioning is a very important component of marketing and economic conditions and city council mood indicated that being an efficient provider of services was highly desirable. By responding to changing conditions in the leisure activities market, a portion of which the library served, Mr. Bradbury could present a solid case for the library becoming a co-ordinator of leisure activities and not just another competitor for funds.

Strategically this new arrangement provided both the city and the library with some satisfaction. The city could toot its horn becuase it was encouraging more cost efficiency and interdepartmental cooperation, and doing so with high visibility services. The library in turn would gain a larger constituency, broader program base and be a greater power to be contended with at city meetings. The citizens would be exposed to less duplication of services such as film programs or bicycle programs being run simultaneously by two departments. The enlarged role of the library would expose many non-users to library service options.

For 1983 the city budget increased overall only 4% above 1982. The library's budget increased by 12% over the 1982 budget amount and Mr. Bradbury's contract to act in the dual capacity was renewed for 1983.

This may not be an appropriate plan for every occasion but it points out that, if the organization is to survive and continue to offer service, then the needs of the public (funders) must be put above personal wishes. Institutions must be adaptive to changing conditions and improve the linkages between themselves and governing bodies. What the future will bring for J.P.L. is now somewhat predictable and as director Bradbury says about the arrangement, "so far, so good."

Lake Villa Public Library District

Lake Villa is a small country town in a resort area of Northern Illinois. Its public library, like many in the area had started as a reading club with a dedicated group of volunteers making it work. In the late sixties the library was housed in a rented tavern with the periodical backfile in the bathroom. The floors creaked under the load of the collection and the patrons who crowded their way through the narrow aisles to search for books. Only one small table was available for patrons and there were no public restrooms. Clearly there was a need for a new library facility but no plans had been made and since the library was a township unit it would have required approval of the town board for any plans for a new building program.

The library had been trying to save a little money each year out of its operating budget in hopes of being able to some day build a new headquarters. So far there was $20,000, which was far short of the needed $1 million to build an adequate structure. The situation facing Lake Villa in 1968 wasn't much different than the problems that faced thousands of small libraries. Yet, there was a solution.

In 1968 a new board member was elected who brought with him a strong background in marketing. A year later the beginnings of a plan were in place. It called for abandoning the attempt to save money for a building and spending it instead on services. The underlying philosophy was to identify the services most wanted by the community and then go all out to provide them. By increasing circulation and service levels a by-product would be greater crowding problems and awareness of the problem by more library users.

A fortunate change in Illinois Law took place around this time which said a township library could hold a referendum to convert to a district which would give the library autonomous taxing authority, within limits. The Lake Villa Library held the referendum and the issue passed overwhelmingly.

Following the referendum a survey was taken to find out a little more about the library's patrons. Where did they come from; work or home? Were they combining the library with another stop? How far did they come? Did they find what they wanted? What hours should the library be open? The location of the library was not near any major shopping and only the post office was in the same block. It was important to assess the habits of patrons in order to learn what strings to tug when the bigger question came later.

It was learned that an investor was interested in putting in a shopping center on some land he owned on the major traffic artery in the township. The investor was approached on behalf of a mayor in the library's service area to feel out a land donation for a potential library site. Discussions followed and when the land owner saw the library's survey results showing that the overwhelming majority of library patrons would go to the library no matter where it was he quickly realized it would be a great drawing card for his shopping center if it was located on his land. He offered to give the library five acres on the main highway if the library board would build a new building on the site.

Before the board accepted this gift it called all the elected officials and asked them to appoint people to serve on a site advisory committee to investigate possible new sites for a building. This committee represented all the political and social interests in the community. The library board president charged them with making a site recommendation and then going back to their respective constituencies and supporting a referendum to fund a bond issue for a new library to be built on the selected site. They agreed and voted to recommend the site being donated by the developer.

The status of the library service in Lake Villa was greatly improved by this point with a 100% increase in funds spent on materials (no savings account for a new building), a 50% increase in open hours, a staff that sensed a change and was very enthusiastic and a community with 73% of its residents holding current library cards. On Saturdays people could barely move inside the old rented tavern.

An architect was retained and renderings were submitted. The board wanted a meeting room, lounging areas, high energy efficiency incorporating passive solar heating, a large children's area and a design so minimal staffing could operate the library. A triangular building with insulation on the exterior was proposed that when combined with a sun wall on the south would be very cheap to heat.

The site selection committee supported it to their communities, the staff talked up its energy innovation to patrons, the papers did stories, and the library did a newsletter mailing to the whole township.

The big question was popped and little Lake Villa township's library patrons said YES to a one million dollar building and a 60% increase in the library budget. The vote was two to one for the library. The plan took six years to accomplish and took library service from part time and inadequate for community needs to a library facility and service level as good as any town its size in the country. This was a marketing plan that: identified the need, determined who could positively influence a solution and how to persuade them to do so, who could lend financial help and how to diffuse possible problems with political entities.

Several key points are worth covering in this example of marketing in a public library setting.

The size of the project and the apparent resources of the community are not the principle concerns. Cold logic can be overcome by emotion and ground swell and even a little rural town can marshall the resources to provide good library service funding if they are presented with a proper plan. The combination of a small tavern with library staff obviously struggling with deplorable conditions and a willing land donor helped to bring the project to fruition. But careful work with all the political and special interests was very critical to success. Spending money wisely on the materials that were most asked for helped insure support from satisfied users and clarified the issue. The board was asking for a new building and not operating funds.

By having a mayor intercede with the developer on behalf of the library it indicated a wider concern and helped acquire the gift. The village, which then had a vested interest, was able to provide concessions to the builder to make his shopping center more economical.

There are different constituencies in each community and it takes time and planning to win them over to your side. Finding their buttons and learning how to push them is lots more effective than pressure. Pressure is simply not compatible with the image of public libraries, but satisfying patron needs is highly compatible. The basis of marketing in this case might be stated as: Find the need and fill it. Ask for your reward and if you were correct about the need and you filled it successfully you will be rewarded.

These cases illustrate in real world examples that marketing principles do work, even in very adverse conditions. Both libraries repositioned. One from a provider of information and recreation services, and the other from a part time reading library to a full service facility offering public areas to many groups previously unserved. Both institutions were using marketing techniques to increase their funding in order to respond to greater service demands from patrons. As a result of these efforts the Janesville staff got raises when other departments in the city got none, and the Lake Villa staff became full time and had compensation increased accordingly. The active recognition of political bodies as an import constituency of these libraries contributed immeasurably to the success of their efforts.

REFERENCES

1. O. Gene Norman, "Marketing Libraries and Information Services: An Annotated Guide to the Literature." RSR (Spring 1982): p. 69-80.

2. Norman, p. 80.

3. Norman's literature review includes 94 citations.

4. Barbara Conroy, "Management and Marketing of Public Services." *Journal of Library Administration,* v. 3(1): (Spring 1982), p. 9-12.

5. John P. Dessauer, "Are Libraries Failing Their Patrons?" *Publishers' Weekly* 217 (January 18, 1983): p. 67-68.

6. John Berry, "The Marketization of Libraries," *Library Journal* 106 (January 1, 1981): p. 5.

7. Dessauer, p. 68.

8. John B. Miner and Norman R. Smith, "Can Organizational Decline Make Up for Motivational Decline?" *The Wharton Magazine,* v. 5(4), Spring 1981, p. 29-35.

9. Miner and Smith, p. 35.

10. Philip Kotler, *Marketing for Nonprofit Organizations,* 2d. ed., Englewood Cliffs, N.J.: Prentice-Hall, 1982, p. 23.

11. Andrea C. Dragon, "The Measurement of Professional Performance: A Critical Review." *Annual Review of Library Administration and Organization.* In press.

Distribution of the Library's Product: The Need for Innovation

Darlene E. Weingand, Ph.D.

Marketing as a conceptual structure was nearly totally unknown to the library community a decade ago. During that decade, Philip Kotler has produced two editions of his landmark work, *Marketing for Nonprofit Organizations,* and libraries, as well as other nonprofit agencies, began to envision potential linkages with what, heretofore, has been regarded as a group of techniques suitable solely for the profit sector.

This breakthrough in administrative thought has opened totally new vistas and opportunities for library interaction with its various communities. This article will attempt to draw relationships between library distribution strategies as currently constituted and some of the possible models for future implementation—with marketing theory as the bridge between them. Although the discussion cites the public library and its community, it is important to note that these models are generalizable, that every type of library and information agency has a community which it serves, and that innovation needs to occur in every aspect of the information industry if the agencies and their clienteles are to effectively cope with a rapidly changing environment.

DISTRIBUTION AS A CONTROLLABLE MARKETING VARIABLE

It has been convenient for marketing scholars to categorize the controllable marketing variables into the four P's: Product, Price, Place and Promotion. The "P" under consideration here is third in this series: "Place". In other words, if the assumption is made that the product is of good quality (for no series of strategies can market an inadequate product for very long), that its benefits are communicated to potential consumers, and that the price to produce the product is equitable for both producer and consumer (and therefore is economically feasible and viable), then the next strategy for consideration is that of distribution (or place).

It must be emphasized that all elements of the marketing mix are important because consumer perception of the product is based on the sum

---

Darlene E. Weingand is Assistant Professor, University of Wisconsin, Madison, Library School.

49

total of these elements. However, distribution is often neglected and yet effective distribution is integral to the total marketing structure. Without well thought out distribution strategies, predicated on client needs, the marketing effort is not balanced and is less likely to be successful.

DISTRIBUTION AS A PART OF THE MARKETING AUDIT

The Marketing Audit is a needs assessment tailored to the function and purpose of determining where the library stands in terms of its marketing strategy, its competition, and the gaps which exist in terms of effective marketing techniques. Current marketing approaches are audited in an attempt to assess current practices and to identify possible improvements in either service or cost of service. (For detailed explanation of the process of the marketing audit, see Kotler, 1975 edition.)

The marketing audit, with its analysis of user needs, present areas of service delivery, duplication and competition, and recommendations for service alterations, is the critical baseline upon which the entire marketing structure is constructed. The implications for distribution can be profound when user need is placed in its position of primary importance.

For example, the marketing audit may find that distribution of library services concentrates on the traditional one-on-one model: librarian and patron/client/user (depending upon current popular jargon). The audit may also find that distribution of library services is conducted primarily through the physical location of the site/building. These two models, the face-to-face interaction model and the concept of the library as a physical place, however rewarding to some librarians and some patrons, cannot be viewed as the only conceivable models for distribution. Consideration must be given to alternatives which meet current and potential patron needs in a more efficient manner. There is fundamentally no rationale for exclusive continuation of these two models except for tradition and a certain sense of personal effectiveness. The inclusion of middlemen and intermediaries, as exemplified by the private sector's use of human and technological distribution channels, can well be adapted in certain circumstances to library operations.

For example, in a community where local industry works around the clock and a cable television franchise has been awarded for an interactive system, the traditional model of a library building which is open 20-50 hours per week may be able to serve only a small portion of the population. If, however, the audit uncovers a high community interest in longer hours and cable access, modifications in building hours and cable interface can be explored.

This is only one example; many more are possible. The opportunities presented in technological intermediaries are enormous and will be discussed in depth. Technology offers entrance into new modes and new patterns of thinking and delivery that may well make fundamental changes in how libraries operate.

Libraries have distribution alternatives on a variety of levels: (1) request and dissemination of information; (2) programmatic activities; (3) user browsing; (4) cooperation with corollary agencies. Each of these levels also has the potential of various channels of distribution, whether the channel be a physical location or an electronic delivery system. Therefore, a "tree" effect can be constructed as the library extends "branches" of distribution toward the needs of its users. The coordination of library administration and service with the multiple levels of potential interface is a challenging task, but one that library administrators must face and learn to do well if the library consumers are to be provided with the best possible service.

Two types of results may occur from this maze of interfacing. First, the consumer's needs are answered with speed and accuracy, if the wide scope of information retrieval is available to the local agency. Second, the requisite funding and cooperation for such retrieval may be achieved through inter-agency and inter-level networking.

It is important to remember that the marketing audit will portray a different scenario to each individual library, but whatever the picture described, there are certain decision problems which must be addressed, with the audit as a baseline of decision-making.

DISTRIBUTION DECISION PROBLEMS

How the library plans to make its services available to its clientele is the crux of the distribution decision. There are many factors to consider, including quality of service, time (and distance), convenience, priorities, format, and client attitude. Considered separately, the following issues emerge.

Quality of Service

Since library service is both product and delivery, it becomes even more imperative to strive for a high level of quality—perhaps the demand for quality will require even a higher standard than required for many products. This may seem circuitous, for it is far easier to think in terms of a concrete product, which libraries have traditionally done by placing the focus on materials and buildings. While these elements are admittedly integral components of library service, the restructuring of emphasis is more than a simple format change; it affects all aspects of library operations, decision-making, staff attitudes, and, ultimately, community perceptions of library mission and purpose.

But what is quality service? In simple terms, it is responding with appropriate speed and accuracy to a user need. Although the concept of quality service is difficult to measure, a step toward this goal was taken by Wind, Grashof and Goldhar in a recent *Journal of Marketing* article. According to Wind et al., "Any product or service can be viewed as a collection of structural, functional, psychological, social and economic attributes." (1978, 27-28)

The list of factors and levels included in their attempt to identify the attributes of service important to special library users included: nature of output; output format; mode of search; speed of obtaining information; distribution; mode of payment; type of supplier; language used for inquiry; purchase arrangement; topical coverage; period coverage; and price/cost.

The use of the technique of "conjoint analysis" allowed the authors to address four key questions: (1) What is the usage of each product attribute? (2) How important is each class of attributes? (3) What tradeoffs can be made? and (4) How do answers to the above questions vary among market segments?

Thus the use of conjoint analysis gives the service provider, in this case the library, a reasonable idea of potential client reaction to various design changes. In addition, it allows diverse groups to be broken out in the research so that market segmentation strategies can become part of the overall experiment.

It is interesting to note that in this cited research, the three most highly valued attributes were: (1) nature of output (from simple citations to citation plus answer to problem); (2) output format (i.e., computer printout, photocopy, verbal, etc.); and (3) speed of obtaining information. (Wind et al., 31) All of these functions relate directly to distribution concerns and underscore the importance of distribution in the total marketing effort.

In addition to this empirical evidence, since monetary support is crucial to the continuance of any product, it is important to remember that there is very little rationale for the expenditure of funds if the monies are not directly incorporated into a service concept. The distribution decision implicit in service is one that merges product quality and ease of access (in terms of desired output and speed). Although the other decision problems also flow into the issue of access, access is paramount in the reality and user perception of service quality and is so central that it must be treated as a primary service goal.

Time, Convenience and Resource Allocation

Since library users value time—particularly in a society where change is accelerating rapidly and information increases geometrically—then needs must be given serious consideration by those who have the power and responsibility of creating more time effective distribution channels.

The less time that a library client is required to spend in pursuit of an information need, the higher the level of service and the degree of potential user satisfaction. The conjoint analysis research cited above, in determining that speed of information was one of the most important system-design factors, discovered that preferred response to an information need was within a working day. (Wind et al., 1978, 32)

Time can be approached from three perspectives: the time expended by library staff to provide the information; the time expended in overcoming the physical distance between user and service; and the real time that library service is available to the user. These perspectives describe a highly important concept: convenience. If the library is convenient to the user, then one aspect of access has been satisfied.

However, in a time of economic retrenchment it is difficult to conceive of distribution channels which can allow significant improvement in user convenience. It can be deemed impossible to lengthen library hours, establish more physical outlets, or add staff in an effort to expedite information handling. These "impossibilities" are, of course, predicated on traditional and limited models of distribution. When financial considerations are addressed, it is vital to incorporate user needs and establishment of priorities based upon those needs into the budgetary process.

Accompanying those traditional models of distribution has been that method of resource allocation which is based on intuition: "an intuition nurtured by library school, developed over years of experience, changed by new inventions, but rarely affected by any formal intervention from the users in the way of an expression of their wants." (Robertson, 1)

Rather than conforming to traditional distribution and resource allocation patterns, what the user wants should drive the ranking of priorities of service, and those clusters of services at the top of the list given primary consideration. This ranking of services based upon user need will result in wide variation of services provided among different types and sizes of libraries. However, this variation is appropriate and is in harmony with the user-oriented approach of current marketing theory.

Planning and Priorities

This concentration on the setting of priorities which reflect user needs must be done within the context of a well thought out and routine planning process. Annual establishment of an operational plan for the coming year, plus updating of a five year long range plan, is the basic framework within which innovative planning can be created.

An important consideration in terms of planning is the concept of "stakeholder management," which was introduced into the planning literature by Ansoff in 1965. In a further amplification of this concept, Davis (1980) examines an approach to planned change which looks at perceived barriers to self-initiated planning and proposes strategic efforts to redefine the relationship between the library and its environment. In this proactive model, Davis reaffirms that "stakeholder planning emphasizes strategic participation of those groups who have an important stake in the institution, and who are willing to search for jointly advantageous solutions to problems" (Davis, 1980, 17). He stresses that:

> For most libraries the (economic) buffer has gone. The library is closely "engaged" with its environment and must adapt itself to it. The days in which a library could move into the future riding on past traditions, buffered by a cushion of slack resources, are over. (Davis, 1980, 20)

Stakeholder management can be implemented through use of a planning committee composed of representatives of the library's various constituency groups, plus internal organizational representatives. The benefits of this continuous input into the planning process far outweigh the added expenditure of staff time which is required. In many ways, working through such a committee is analogous to having an on-going marketing audit: the continuous input data and communication linkages can help the administration to closely monitor the pulse of the community.

This monitoring is advantageous to all elements of the marketing effort, but the information gleaned in terms of distribution channels can be particularly welcome. As community conditions change, as library user needs ebb and flow in rhythm with these changing conditions, many signals can be picked up via the knowledge of this type of committee. In addition, the notion of clients being directly involved in structuring response to their needs fits well with this whole model of user-oriented marketing.

Effective Use of Human Resource Intermediaries

Opportunities exist in the expansion of available human resources. These opportunities may include: 1) Cooperation with corollary human service and governmental agencies in terms of joint programs, information and referral, and sharing of physical resources. 2) Contractual agreements with service brokers, such as private information entrepreneurs, to provide those specific functions to which the library may be unwilling or unable to commit existing staff. 3) Development of a dynamic volunteer program to provide service to those clients physically unable through disability or age to contact an existing service outlet (such as Books by Mail, Books on Tape, or homebound service). These measures are not startling, but they are also not always considered as alternatives in service delivery. Manipulation of the planning process to include the widest variety of alternatives is a challenging effort, and one increasingly worth doing.

Number and Location of Outlets

Tied directly to the setting of priorities is the examination of existing and potential service outlets. It has been an historically difficult experience to attempt to close a branch or outlet which has suffered decreasing use. It has been correspondingly difficult to initiate the sense of adventure and innovation required to secure funding and support for the implementation of alternative outlets, such as portable structures/kiosks (either free-standing or in cooperating sites, such as grocery stores or skyways) and telecommunications delivery systems.

User-oriented marketing and planning strategies can frequently smooth the approach to these alternative modes of service delivery. Outlets are, in basic terms, the points of intersection between user and product. Each type of point needs to reflect the needs of the market segment it purports to serve. Traditional groupings of clients may no longer be practical in this changing society as technology, career paths, educational backgrounds and needs, and shifting political boundaries create new patterns of human growth and interaction. This potentially changing nature of the library's client structure suggests that market segmentation—the concentration on sub-groups which have more homogeneous characteristics than the whole—may be a useful strategy. This would involve on-going market research and contact with identified segments, but also the additional strategy of testing prototype products to determine where and how needs can actually be met.

Format and Technology

Probably the most challenging and threatening potentiality lies in the use of appropriate format and technology to deliver information. Human intelligence is busily engaged in the creation and development of increasingly sophisticated communications devices. Time and distance are no longer significant factors as the utilization of telecommunications technology renders them meaningless as obstacles to user convenience.

Format can be considered in two aspects: 1) As media format—i.e., video, audio, film, microform, computer software, or print—which can be host to information content, 2) As structure for service delivery—i.e., communications channels, which may take the form of cable television, interactive video and/or computer networks, teleconferencing networks, broadcasting systems, satellite transmission, videotex—and permutations and combinations of these modes. The point to be made is that while the library's service product flows with community need and within the standards of excellence, the library's service delivery system can have great and increasing flexibility if it has sufficient mobility of capital to adopt new forms. Innovation in terms of channels of distribution allows new alternatives and options to continually emerge, but these channels must be developed in correlation with what users and potential users want.

For example, the approaches used by Standard and Poor's Corporation to distribute information electronically vary almost as widely as the scope of information services available in the marketplace (Newcomb, 1983, 152). This variation directly reflects the corresponding clientele variation and information use, and can provide a model for study by the public sector.

Consider a scenario: For maximum user convenience, access to information should be available twenty-four hours per day. There are few, if any, libraries that could afford the cost of staffing such a service goal; such access is obviously beyond the realm of reality. But is it? What if the entire notion of library service being directly tied to an open physical site with adequate staff support is temporarily suspended. In its place, insert a new structure:

1. The physical service outlets are open for direct use during present (or reduced) hours. Typically, this will range between four and twelve hours per day.

2. As a complement to this direct use model, the local cable television network offers an interactive system whereby citizens can interact with the library's catalog and/or reference service from the comfort of home. (Pilot projects have occurred via Channel 2000 in Columbus, OH; Maggie's Place in Pike's Peak, CO; and the Iowa City, IA Public Library. Advances in videotex experimentation will increase the potential for additional library involvement across the nation in the next decade.)

3. When the library's physical outlets close for the day, the cable network remains operative—through the totality of the day—and library staff take turns working "swing shift" hours, serving as resources to the community via the interactive cable set-up. The result, of course, is twenty-four hour library access through the creation of a new and innovative service model. Impossible? Not at all . . .

Newcomb (1983, 155), in an analysis of electronic information distribution in the publishing industry, sees the challenge as "an attempt to solve a new and complex puzzle with numerous interrelated parts: evaluating the changing information demands within traditional markets and emerging new markets; determining the appropriate distribution vehicle; deciding whether to build the necessary distribution capability or enter into a joint venture; making complex pricing judgments; and changing . . . focuses." A prescription such as this requires rethinking and a willingness to risk. It is important, moreover, that an organization should consciously choose how it positions itself in its marketplace (Sterngold, 1982, 255), with decisions made concerning which target groups and which information needs will be satisfied—and through what channels of distribution.

Innovation in channels of distribution is only bound by the limits of imagination, creativity, and money. When correlated to community information needs, these diverse channels could make the library truly responsive to what the community requires for coping and learning. When information access is ever-present, and marketing pricing and promotional strategies encourage citizen participation, then the library may finally achieve the long-espoused goal of being the communication and information center of the community it serves. Clients may, at last, regard the library as an essential service. This positive client attitude toward the library can lead into implementation of a funding structure that allows for continued expansion of service—both product and channels.

Of the "4 P's" of the Marketing Method, distribution is frequently given the least direct attention. However, for those seeking to affect the library's future in an innovative manner, the possibilities of creative distribution offer a real challenge and, perhaps, the "best shot" at effectively dealing with tomorrow's world.

REFERENCES

Davis, Peter. "Libraries at the Turning Point: Issues in Proactive Planning." *Journal of Library Administration.* 1:2 (Summer 1980), 11-24.

Kotler, Philip. *Marketing for Nonprofit Organizations.* Englewood Cliffs, NJ: Prentice-Hall, 1975. 2nd ed., 1982.

Newcomb, J. "Electronic Information Distribution," *Special Libraries,* 74:2(April 1983), 150-155.

Robertson, W. Davenport. "A User-Oriented Approach to Setting Priorities for Library Services," (unpublished paper presented at the Special Library Association Conference, Honolulu, Hawaii, June 1979)

Sterngold, Arthur. "Marketing for Special Libraries and Information Centers: The Positioning Process," *Special Libraries.* 73:4(October 1982), 254-259.

Weingand, Darlene E., ed. *Marketing for Libraries: A Reader.* Norwood, NJ: Ablex Publishing Corporation (in process)

Wind, Yoram, John F. Grashof and Joel D. Goldbar. "Market Based Guidelines for Design of Industrial Products; A New Application of Conjoint Analysis to Scientific and Technical Information (STI) Services," *Journal of Marketing.* 42:3(July 1978), 27-37.

Marketing Myopia

Theodore Levitt

Every major industry was once a growth industry. But some that are now riding a wave of growth enthusiasm are very much in the shadow of decline. Others which are thought of as seasoned growth industries have actually stopped growing. In every case the reason growth is threatened, slowed, or stopped is *not* because the market is saturated. It is because there has been a failure of management.

FATEFUL PURPOSES

The failure is at the top. The executives responsible for it, in the last analysis, are those who deal with broad aims and policies. Thus:

> The railroads did not stop growing because the need for passenger and freight transportation declined. That grew. The railroads are in trouble today not because the need was filled by others (cars, trucks, airplanes, even telephones), but because it was *not* filled by the railroads themselves. They let others take customers away from them because they assumed themselves to be in the railroad business rather than in the transportation business. The reason they defined their industry wrong was because they were railroad-oriented instead of transportation-oriented; they were product-oriented instead of customer-oriented.
>
> Hollywood barely escaped being totally ravished by television. Actually, all the established film companies went through drastic reorganizations. Some simply disappeared. All of them got into trouble not because of TV's inroads but because of their own myopia. As with the railroads, Hollywood defined its business incorrectly. It thought it was in the movie business when it was actually in the entertainment business. "Movies" implied a specific, limited product. This produced a fatuous contentment which from the beginning led producers to view TV as a threat. Hollywood scorned and rejected TV when it should have welcomed it as an opportunity—an opportunity to expand the entertainment business.

Today TV is a bigger business than the old narrowly defined movie business ever was. Had Hollywood been customer-oriented (providing entertainment), rather than product-oriented (making movies), would it have gone through the fiscal purgatory that it did? I doubt it. What ultimately saved Hollywood and accounted for its recent resurgence was the wave of new young writers, producers, and directors whose previous successes in television had decimated the old movie companies and toppled the big movie moguls.

There are other less obvious examples of industries that have been and are now endangering their futures by improperly defining their purposes. I shall discuss some in detail later and analyze the kind of policies that lead to trouble. Right now it may help to show what a thoroughly customer-oriented management *can* do to keep a growth industry growing, even after the obvious opportunities have been exhausted; and here there are two examples that have been around for a long time. They are nylon and glass—specifically, E.I. dePont de Nemours & Company and Corning Glass Works:

Both companies have great technical competence. Their product orientation is unquestioned. But this alone does not explain their success. After all, who was more pridefully product-oriented and product-conscious than the erstwhile New England textile companies that have been so thoroughly massacred? The DuPonts and the Cornings have succeeded not primarily because of their product or research orientation but because they have been thoroughly customer-oriented also. It is constant watchfulness for opportunities to apply their technical know-how to the creation of customer-satisfying uses which accounts for their prodigious output of successful new products. Without a very sophisticated eye on the customer, most of their new products might have been wrong, their sales methods useless.

Aluminum has also continued to be a growth industry, thanks to the efforts of two wartime-created companies which deliberately set about creating new customer-satisfying uses. Without Kaiser Aluminum & Chemical Corporation and Reynolds Metals Company, the total demand for aluminum today would be vastly less than it is.

Error of Analysis

Some may argue that it is foolish to set the railroads off against aluminum or the movies off against glass. Are not aluminum and glass naturally so versatile that the industries are bound to have more growth opportunities than the railroads and movies? This view commits precisely the error I have been talking about. It defines an industry, or a product, or a cluster of knowhow so narrowly as to guarantee its premature senescence. When we mention "railroads," we should make sure we mean "transportation." As transporters, the railroads still have a good chance for very considerable growth. They are not limited to the railroad business as such (though in my opinion rail transportation is potentially a much stronger transportation medium than is generally believed).

What the railroads lack is not opportunity, but some of the same managerial imaginativeness and audacity that made them great. Even an amateur like Jacques Barzun can see what is lacking when he says:

> "I grieve to see the most advanced physical and social organization of the last century go down in shabby disgrace for lack of the same comprehensive imagination that built it up. [What is lacking is] the will of the companies to survive and to satisfy the public by inventiveness and skill."[1]

SHADOW OF OBSOLESCENCE

It is impossible to mention a single major industry that did not at one time qualify for the magic appellation of "growth industry." In each case its assumed strength lay in the apparently unchallenged superiority of its product. There appeared to be no effective substitute for it. It was itself a runaway substitute for the product it so triumphantly replaced. Yet one after another of these celebrated industries has come under a shadow. Let us look briefly at a few more of them, this time taking examples that have so far received a little less attention:

> *Dry cleaning*—This was once a growth industry with lavish prospects. In an age of wool garments, imagine being finally able to get them safely and easily clean. The boom was on.
>
> Yet here we are 30 years after the boom started and the industry is in trouble. Where has the competition come from? From a better way of cleaning? No. It has come from synthetic fibers and chemical additives that have cut the need for dry cleaning. But this is only the beginning. Lurking in the wings and ready to make chemical dry cleaning totally obsolescent is that powerful magician, ultrasonics.
>
> *Electric utilities*—This is another one of those supposedly "no-substitute" products that has been enthroned on a pedestal of invincible growth. When the incandescent lamp came along, kerosene lights were finished. Later the water wheel and the steam engine were cut to ribbons by the flexibility, reliability, simplicity, and just

plain easy availability of electric motors. The prosperity of electric utilities continues to wax extravagent as the home is converted into a museum of electric gadgetry. How can anybody miss by investing in utilities, with no competition, nothing but growth ahead?

But a second look is not quite so comforting. A score of nonutility companies are well advanced toward developing a powerful chemical fuel cell which could sit in some hidden closet of every home silently ticking off electric power. The electric lines that vulgarize so many neighborhoods will be eliminated. So will the endless demolition of streets and service interruptions during storms. Also on the horizon is solar energy, again pioneered by nonutility companies.

Who says that the utilities have no competition? They may be natural monopolies now, but tomorrow they may be natural deaths. To avoid this prospect, they too will have to develop fuel cells, solar energy, and other power sources. To survive, they themselves will have to plot the obsolescence of what now produces their livelihood.

Grocery stores—Many people find it hard to realize that there ever was a thriving establishment known as the "corner grocery store." The supermarket has taken over with a powerful effectiveness. Yet the big food chains of the 1930s narrowly escaped being completely wiped out by the aggressive expansion of independent supermarkets. The first genuine supermarket was opened in 1930, in Jamaica, Long Island. By 1933 supermarkets were thriving in California, Ohio, Pennsylvania, and elsewhere. Yet the established chains pompously ignored them. When they chose to notice them, it was with such derisive descriptions as "cheapy," "horse-and-buggy," "cracker-barrel storekeeping," and "unethical opportunists."

The executive of one big chain announced at the time that he found it "hard to believe that people will drive for miles to shop for foods and sacrifice the personal service chains have perfected and to which Mrs. Consumer is accustomed."[2] As late as 1936, the National Wholesale Grocers convention and the New Jersey Retail Grocers Association said there was nothing to fear. They said that the supers' narrow appeal to the price buyer limited the size of their market. They had to draw from miles around. When imitators came, there would be wholesale liquidations as volume fell. The current high sales of the supers was said to be partly due to their novelty. Basically people wanted convenient neighborhood grocers. If the neighborhood stores "cooperate with their suppliers, pay attention to their costs, and improve their service," they would be able to weather the competition until it blew over.[3]

It never blew over. The chains discovered that survival required going into the supermarket business. This meant the wholesale destruction of their huge investments in corner store sites and in established distribution and merchandising methods. The companies with "the courage of their convictions" resolutely stuck to the corner store philosophy. They kept their pride but lost their shirts.

Self-Deceiving Cycle

But memories are short. For example, it is hard for people who today confidently hail the twin messiahs of electronics and chemicals to see how things could possibly go wrong with these galloping industries. They probably also cannot see how a reasonably sensible businessman could have been as myopic as the famous Boston millionaire who 50 years ago unintentionally sentenced his heirs to poverty by stipulating that his entire estate be forever invested exclusively in electric streetcar securities. His posthumous declaration, "There will always be a big demand for efficient urban transportation," is no consolation to his heirs who sustain life by pumping gasoline at automobile filling stations.

Yet, in a casual survey I recently took among a group of intelligent business executives, nearly half agreed that it would be hard to hurt their heirs by tying their estates forever to the electronics industry. When I then confronted them with the Boston streetcar example, they chorused unanimously, "That's different!" But is it? Is not the basic situation identical?

In truth, *there is no such thing* as a growth industry, I believe. There are only companies organized and operated to create and capitalize on growth opportunities. Industries that assume themselves to be riding some automatic growth escalator invariably descend into stagnation. The history of every dead and dying "growth" industry shows a self-deceiving cycle of bountiful expansion and undetected decay. There are four conditions which usually guarantee this cycle:

1. The belief that growth is assured by an expanding and more affluent population.
2. The belief that there is no competitive substitute for the industry's major product.
3. Too much faith in mass production and in the advantages of rapidly declining unit costs as output rises.
4. Preoccupation with a product that lends itself to carefully controlled scientific experimentation, improvement, and manufacturing cost reduction.

I should like now to begin examining each of these conditions in some detail. To build my case as boldly as possible, I shall illustrate the points with reference to three industries—petroleum, automobiles, and electronics—particularly petroleum, because it spans more years and more vicissitudes. Not only do these three have excellent reputations with the general public and also enjoy the confidence of sophisticated investors, but their managements have become known for progressive thinking in areas like financial control, product research, and management training. If obsolescence can cripple even these industries, it can happen anywhere.

POPULATION MYTH

The belief that profits are assured by an expanding and more affluent population is dear to the heart of every industry. It takes the edge off the apprehensions everybody understandably feels about the future. If consumers are multiplying and also buying more of your product or service, you can face the future with considerably more comfort than if the market is shrinking. An expanding market keeps the manufacturer from having to think very hard or imaginatively. If thinking is an intellectual response to a problem, then the absence of a problem leads to the absence of thinking. If your product has an automatically expanding market, then you will not give much thought to how to expand it.

One of the most interesting examples of this is provided by the petroleum industry. Probably our oldest growth industry, it has an enviable record. While there are some current apprehensions about its growth rate, the industry itself tends to be optimistic. But I believe it can be demonstrated that it is undergoing a fundamental yet typical change. It is not only ceasing to be a growth industry, but may actually be a declining one, relative to other business. Although there is widespread unawareness of it, I believe that within 25 years the oil industry may find itself in much the same position of retrospective glory that the railroads are now in. Despite its pioneering work in developing and applying the present-value method of investment evaluation, in employee relations, and in working with backward countries, the petroleum business is a distressing example of how complacency and wrongheadedness can stubbornly convert opportunity into near disaster.

One of the characteristics of this and other industries that have believed very strongly in the beneficial consequences of an expanding population, while at the same time being industries with a generic product for which there has appeared to be no competitive substitute, is that the individual companies have sought to outdo their competitors by improving on what they are already doing. This makes sense, of course, if one assumes that sales are tied to the country's population strings, because the customer can compare products only on a feature-by-feature basis. I believe it is significant, for example, that not since John D. Rockefeller sent free kerosene lamps to China has the oil industry done anything really outstanding to create a demand for its product. Not even in product improvement has it showered itself with eminence. The greatest single improvement, namely, the development of tetraethyl lead, came from outside the industry, specifically from General Motors and DuPont. The big contributions made by the industry itself are confined to the technology of oil exploration, production, and refining.

Asking for Trouble

In other words, the industry's efforts have focused on improving the *efficiency* of getting and making its product, not really on improving the generic product or its marketing. Moreover, its chief product has continuously been defined in the narrowest possible terms, namely, gasoline, not energy, fuel, or transportation. This attitude has helped assure that:

> Major improvements in gasoline quality tend not to originate in the oil industry. Also, the development of superior alternative fuels comes from outside the oil industry, as will be shown later.
>
> Major innovations in automobile fuel marketing are originated by small new oil companies that are not primarily preoccupied with production or refining. These are the companies that have been responsible for the rapidly expanding multipump gasoline stations, with their successful emphasis on large and clean layouts, rapid and efficient driveway service, and quality gasoline at low prices.

Thus, the oil industry is asking for trouble from outsiders. Sooner or later, in this land of hungry inventors and entrepreneurs, a threat is sure to come. The possibilities of this will become more apparent when we turn to the next dangerous belief of many managements. For the sake of continuity, because this second belief is tied closely to the first, I shall continue with the same example.

Idea of Indispensability

The petroleum industry is pretty much persuaded that there is no competitive substitute for its major product, gasoline—or if there is, that it will continue to be a derivative of crude oil, such as diesel fuel or kerosene jet fuel.

There is a lot of automatic wishful thinking in this assumption. The trouble is that most refining companies own huge amounts of crude oil reserves. These have value only if there is a market for products into which oil can be converted—hence the tenacious belief in the continuing competitive superiority of automobile fuels made from crude oil.

This idea persists despite all historic evidence against it. The evidence not only shows that oil has never been a superior product for any purpose for very long, but it also shows that the oil industry has never really been a growth industry. It has been a succession of different businesses that have gone through the usual historic cycles of growth, maturity, and decay. Its over-all survival is owed to a series of miraculous escapes from total obsolescence, of last-minute and unexpected reprieves from total disaster reminiscent of the Perils of Pauline.

Perils of Petroleum

I shall sketch in only the main episodes:
First, crude oil was largely a patent medicine. But even before that fad ran out, demand was greatly expanded by the use of oil in kerosene lamps. The prospect of lighting the world's lamps gave rise to an extravagant promise of growth. The prospects were similar to those the industry now holds for gasoline in other parts of the world. It can hardly wait for the underdeveloped nations to get a car in every garage.

In the days of the kerosene lamp, the oil companies competed with each other and against gaslight by trying to improve the illuminating characteristics of kerosene. Then suddenly the impossible happened. Edison invented a light which was totally nondependent on crude oil. Had it not been for the growing use of kerosene in space heaters, the incandescent lamp would have completely finished oil as a growth industry at that time. Oil would have been good for little else than axle grease.

Then disaster and reprieve struck again. Two great innovations occurred, neither originating in the oil industry. The successful development of coal-burning domestic central-heating systems made the space heater obsolescent. While the industry reeled, along came its most magnificent boost yet—the internal combustion engine, also invented by outsiders. Then when the prodigious expansion for gasoline finally began to level off in the 1920s, along came the miraculous escape of a central oil heater. Once again, the escape was provided by an outsider's invention and development. And when that market weakened, wartime demand for aviation fuel came to the rescue. After the war the expansion of civilian aviation, the dieselization of railroads, and the explosive demand for cars and trucks kept the industry's growth in high gear.

Meanwhile centralized oil heating—whose boom potential had only recently been proclaimed—ran into severe competition from natural gas. While the oil companies themselves owned the gas that now competed with their oil, the industry did not originate the natural gas revolution, nor has it to this day greatly profited from its gas ownership. The gas revolution was made by newly formed transmission companies that marketed the product with an aggressive ardor. They started a magnificent new industry, first against the advice and then against the resistance of the oil companies.

By all the logic of the situation, the oil companies themselves should have made the gas revolution. They not only owned the gas; they also were the only people experienced in handling, scrubbing, and using it, the only people experienced in pipeline technology and transmission, and they understood heating problems. But, partly because they knew that natural gas would compete with their own sale of heating oil, the oil companies pooh-poohed the potentials of gas.

The revolution was finally started by oil pipeline executives who, unable to persuade their own companies to go into gas, quit and organized the spectacularly successful gas transmission companies. Even after their success became painfully evident to the oil companies, the latter did not go into gas transmission. The multibillion dollar business which should have been theirs went to others. As in the past, the industry was blinded by its narrow preoccupation with a specific product and the value of its reserves. It paid little or no attention to its customers' basic needs and preferences.

The postwar years have not witnessed any change. Immediately after World War II the oil industry was greatly encouraged about its future by the rapid expansion of demand for its traditional line of products. In 1950 most companies projected annual rates of domestic expansion of around 6% through at least 1975. Though the ratio of crude oil reserves to demand in the Free World was about 20 to 1, with 10 to 1 being usually considered a reasonable working ratio in the United States, booming demand sent oil men searching for more without sufficient regard to what the future really promised. In 1952 they "hit" in the Middle East; the ratio skyrocketed to 42 to 1. If gross additions to reserves continue at the average rate of the past five years (37 billion barrels annually), then by 1970 the reserve ratio will be up to 45 to 1. This abundance of oil has weakened crude and product prices all over the world.

Uncertain Future

Management cannot find much consolation today in the rapidly expanding petrochemical industry, another oil-using idea that did not originate in the leading firms. The total United States production of petrochemicals is equivalent to about 2% (by volume) of the demand for all petroleum products. Although the petrochemical industry is now expected to grow by about 10% per year, this will not offset other drains on the growth of crude oil consumption. Furthermore, while petrochemical products are many and growing, it is well to remember that there are nonpetroleum sources of the basic raw material, such as coal. Besides, a lot of plastics can be produced with relatively little oil. A 50,000-barrel-per-day oil refinery is now considered the absolute minimum size for efficiency. But a 5,000-barrel-per-day chemical plant is a giant operation.

Oil has never been a continuously strong growth industry. It has grown by fits and starts, always miraculously saved by innovations and developments not of its own making. The reason it has not grown in a smooth progression is that each time it thought it had a superior product safe from the possibility of competitive substitutes, the product turned out to be inferior and notoriously subject to obsolescence. Until now, gasoline (for motor fuel, anyhow) has escaped this fate. But, as we shall see later, it too may be on its last legs.

The point of all this is that there is no guarantee against product obsolescence. If a company's own research does not make it obsolete, another's will. Unless an industry is especially lucky, as oil has been until now, it can easily go down in a sea of red figures—just as the railroads have, as the buggy whip manufacturers have, as the corner grocery chains have, as most of the big movie companies have, and indeed as many other industries have.

The best way for a firm to be lucky is to make its own luck. That requires knowing what makes a business successful. One of the greatest enemies of this knowledge is mass production.

PRODUCTION PRESSURES

Mass-production industries are impelled by a great drive to produce all they can. The prospect of steeply declining unit costs as output rises is more than most companies can usually resist. The profit possibilities look spectacular. All effort focuses on production. The result is that marketing gets neglected.

John Kenneth Galbraith contends that just the opposite occurs.[4] Output is so prodigious that all effort concentrates on trying to get rid of it. He says this accounts for singing commercials, desecration of the countryside with advertising signs, and other wasteful and vulgar practices. Galbraith has a finger on something real, but he misses the strategic point. Mass production does indeed generate great pressure to "move" the product. But what usually gets emphasized is selling, not marketing. Marketing, being a more sophisticated and complex process, gets ignored.

The difference between marketing and selling is more than semantic. Selling focuses on the needs of the seller, marketing on the needs of the buyer. Selling is preoccupied with the seller's need to convert his product into cash; marketing with the idea of satisfying the needs of the customer by means of the product and the whole cluster of things associated with creating, delivering, and finally consuming it.

In some industries the enticements of full mass production have been so powerful that for many years top management in effect has told the sales departments, "You get rid of it; we'll worry about profits." By contrast, a truly marketing-minded firm tries to create value-satisfying goods and services that consumers will want to buy. What it offers for sale includes not only the generic product or service, but also how it is made available to the customer, in what form, when, under what conditions, and at what terms of trade. Most important, what it offers for sale is determined not by the seller but by the buyer. The seller takes his cues from the buyer in such a way that the product becomes a consequence of the marketing effort, not vice versa.

Lag in Detroit

This may sound like an elementary rule of business, but that does not keep it from being violated wholesale. It is certainly more violated than honored. Take the automobile industry:

> Here mass production is most famous, most honored, and has the greatest impact on the entire society. The industry has hitched its fortune to the relentless requirements of the annual model change, a policy that makes customer orientation an especially urgent necessity. Consequently the auto companies annually spend millions of dollars on consumer research. But the fact that the new compact cars are selling so well in their first year indicates that Detroit's vast researchers have for a long time failed to reveal what the customer really wanted. Detroit was not persuaded that he wanted anything different from what he had been getting until it lost millions of customers to other small car manufacturers.

> How could this unbelievable lag behind consumer wants have been perpetuated so long? Why did not research reveal consumer preferences before consumers' buying decisions themselves revealed the facts? Is that not what consumer research is for—to find out before the fact what is going to happen? The answer is that Detroit never really researched the customer's wants. It only researched his preferences between the kinds of things which it had already decided to offer him. For Detroit is mainly product-oriented, not customer-oriented. To the extent that the customer is recognized as having needs that the manufacturer should try to satisfy, Detroit usually acts as if the job can be done entirely by product changes. Occasionally attention gets paid to financing, too, but that is done more in order to sell than to enable the customer to buy.

> As for taking care of other customer needs, there is not enough being done to write about. The areas of the greatest unsatisfied

needs are ignored, or at best get stepchild attention. These are at the point of sale and on the matter of automotive repair and maintenance. Detroit views these problem areas as being of secondary importance. That is underscored by the fact that the retailing and servicing ends of this industry are neither owned and operated nor controlled by the manufacturers. Once the car is produced, things are pretty much in the dealer's inadequate hands. Illustrative of Detroit's arm's-length attitude is the fact that, while servicing holds enormous sales-stimulating, profit-building opportunities, only 57 of Chevrolet's 7,000 dealers provide night maintenance service.

Motorists repeatedly express their dissatisfaction with servicing and their apprehensions about buying cars under the present selling setup. The anxieties and problems they encounter during the auto buying and maintenance processes are probably more intense and widespread today than 30 years ago. But the automobile companies do not *seem* to listen to or take their cues from the anguished consumer. If they do listen, it must be through the filter of their own preoccupation with production. The marketing effort is still viewed as a necessary consequence of the product, not vice versa, as it should be. That is the legacy of mass production, with its parochial view that profit resides essentially in low-cost full production.

What Ford Put First

The profit lure of mass production obviously has a place in the plans and strategy of business management, but it must always *follow* hard thinking about the customer. This is one of the most important lessons that we can learn from the contradictory behavior of Henry Ford. In a sense Ford was both the most brilliant and the most senseless marketer in American history. He was senseless because he refused to give the customer anything but a black car. He was brilliant because he fashioned a production system designed to fit market needs. We habitually celebrate him for the wrong reason, his production genius. His real genius was marketing. We think he was able to cut his selling price and therefore sell millions of $500 cars because his invention of the assembly line had reduced the costs. Actually he invented the assembly line because he had concluded that at $500 he could sell millions of cars. Mass production was the *result* not the cause of his low prices.

Ford repeatedly emphasized this point, but a nation of production-oriented business managers refuses to hear the great lesson he taught. Here is his operating philosophy as he expressed it succinctly:

"Our policy is to reduce the price, extend the operations, and improve the article. You will notice that the reduction of price comes first. We have never considered any costs as fixed. Therefore we first reduce the price to the point where we believe more sales will result. Then we go ahead and try to make the prices. We do not bother about the costs. The new price forces the costs down. The more usual way is to take the costs and then determine the price, and although that method may be scientific in the narrow sense; it is not scientific in the broad sense, because what earthly use is it to know the cost if it tells you that you cannot manufacture at a price at which the article can be sold? But more to the point is the fact that, although one may calculate what a cost is, and of course all of our costs are carefully calculated, no one knows what a cost ought to be. One of the ways of discovering . . . is to name a price so low as to force everybody in the place to the highest point of efficiency. The low price makes everybody dig for profits. We make more discoveries concerning manufacturing and selling under this forced method than by any method of leisurely investigation.''[5]

Product Provincialism

The tantalizing profit possibilities of low unit production costs may be the most seriously self-deceiving attitude that can afflict a company, particularly a "growth" company where an apparently assured expansion of demand already tends to undermine a proper concern for the importance of marketing and the customer.

The usual result of this narrow preoccupation with so-called concrete matters is that instead of growing, the industry declines. It usually means that the product fails to adapt to the constantly changing patterns of consumer needs and tastes, to new and modified marketing institutions and practices, or to product developments in competing or complementary industries. The industry has its eyes so firmly on its own specific product that it does not see how it is being made obsolete.

The classical example of this is the buggy whip industry. No amount of product improvement could stave off its death sentence. But had the industry defined itself as being in the transportation business rather than the buggy whip business, it might have survived. It would have done what survival always entails, that is, changing. Even if it had only defined its business as providing a stimulant or catalyst to an energy source, it might have survived by becoming a manufacturer of, say, fanbelts or air cleaners.

What may some day be a still more classical example is, again, the oil industry. Having let others steal marvelous opportunities from it (e.g., natural gas, as already mentioned, missile fuels, and jet engine lubricants), one would expect it to have taken steps never to let that happen again. But this is not the case. We are now getting extraordinary new developments in fuel systems specifically designed to power automobiles. Not only are these developments concentrated in firms outside the petroleum industry, but petroleum is almost systematically ignoring them, securely content in its wedded bliss to oil. It is the story of the kerosene lamp versus the incandescent lamp all over again. Oil is trying to improve hydrocarbon fuels rather than to develop *any* fuels best suited to the needs of their users, whether or not made in different ways and with different raw materials from oil.

Here are some of the things which nonpetroleum companies are working on:

> Over a dozen such firms now have advanced working models of energy systems which, when perfected, will replace the internal combustion engine and eliminate the demand for gasoline. The superior merit of each of these systems is their elimination of frequent, time-consuming, and irritating refueling stops. Most of these systems are fuel cells designed to create electrical energy directly from chemicals without combustion. Most of them use chemicals that are not derived from oil, generally hydrogen and oxygen.
>
> Several other companies have advanced models of electric storage batteries designed to power automobiles. One of these is an aircraft producer that is working jointly with several electric utility companies. The latter hope to use off-peak generating capacity to supply overnight plug-in battery regeneration. Another company, also using the battery approach, is a medium-size electronics firm with extensive small-battery experience that it developed in connection with its work on hearing aids. It is collaborating with an automobile manufacturer. Recent improvements arising from the need for high-powered miniature power storage plants in rockets have put us within reach of a relatively small battery capable of withstanding great overloads or surges of power. Germanium diode applications and batteries using sintered-plate and nickel-cadmium techniques promise to make a revolution in our energy sources.
>
> Solar energy conversion systems are also getting increasing attention. One usually cautions Detroit auto executive recently ventured that solar-powered cars might be common by 1980.

As for the oil companies, they are more or less "watching developments," as one research director put it to me. A few are doing a bit of research on fuel cells, but almost always confined to developing cells powered by hydrocarbon chemicals. None of them are enthusiastically researching fuel cells, batteries, or solar power plants. None of them are spending a fraction as much on research in these profoundly important areas as they are on the usual run-of-the-mill things like reducing combustion chamber deposit in gasoline engines. One major integrated petroleum company recently took a tentative look at the fuel cell and concluded that although "the companies actively working on it indicate a belief in ultimate success . . . the timing and magnitude of its impact are too remote to warrant recognition in our forecasts."

One might, of course, ask: Why should the oil companies do anything different? Would not chemical fuel cells, batteries, or solar energy kill the present product lines? The answer is that they would indeed, and that is precisely the reason for the oil firms having to develop these power units before their competitors, so they will not be companies without an industry.

Management might be more likely to do what is needed for its own preservation if it thought of itself as being in the energy business. But even that would not be enough if it persists in imprisoning itself in the narrow grip of its tight product orientation. It has to think of itself as taking care of customer needs, not finding, refining, or even selling oil. Once it genuinely thinks of its business as taking care of people's transportation needs, nothing can stop it from creating its own extravagantly profitable growth.

"Creative Destruction"

Since words are cheap and deeds are dear, it may be appropriate to indicate what this kind of thinking involves and leads to. Let us start at the beginning—the customer. It can be shown that motorists strongly dislike the bother, delay, and experience of buying gasoline. People actually do not buy gasoline. They cannot see it, taste it, feel it, appreciate it, or really test it. What they buy is the right to continue driving their cars. The gas station is like a tax collector to whom people are compelled to pay a periodic toll as the price of using their cars. This makes the gas station a basically unpopular institution. It can never be made popular or pleasant, only less unpopular, less unpleasant.

To reduce its unpopularity completely means eliminating it. Nobody likes a tax collector, not even a pleasantly cheerful one. Nobody likes to interrupt a trip to buy a phantom product, not even from a handsome Adonis or a seductive Venus. Hence, companies that are working on exotic fuel substitutes which will eliminate the need for frequent refueling are heading directly into the outstretched arms of the irritated motorist. They are riding a wave of inevitability, not because they are creating something which is technologically superior or more sophisticated, but because they are satisfying a powerful customer need. They are also eliminating noxious odors and air pollution.

Once the petroleum companies recognize the customer-satisfying logic of what another power system can do, they will see that they have no more choice about working on an efficient, long-lasting fuel (or some way of delivering present fuels without bothering the motorist) than the big food chains had a choice about getting into the supermarket business, or the vacuum tube companies had a choice about making semiconductors. For their own good the oil firms will have to destroy their own highly profitable assets. No amount of wishful thinking can save them from the necessity of engaging in this form of "creative destruction."

I phrase the need as strongly as this because I think management must make quite an effort to break itself loose from conventional ways. It is all too easy in this day and age for a company or industry to let its sense of purpose become dominated by the economics of full production and to develop a dangerously lopsided product orientation. In short, if management lets itself drift, it invariably drifts in the direction of thinking of itself as producing goods and services, not customer satisfactions. While it probably will not descend to the depths of telling its salesmen, "You get rid of it; we'll worry about profits," it can, without knowing it, be practicing precisely that formula for withering decay. The historic fate of one growth industry after another has been its suicidal product provincialism.

DANGERS OF R & D

Another big danger to a firm's continued growth arises when top management is wholly transfixed by the profit possibilities of technical research and development. To illustrate I shall turn first to a new industry—electronics—and then return once more to the oil companies. By comparing a fresh example with a familiar one, I hope to emphasize the prevalence and insidiousness of a hazardous way of thinking.

Marketing Shortchanged

In the case of electronics, the greatest danger which faces the glamorous new companies in this field is not that they do not pay enough attention to research and development, but that they pay *too much* attention to it. And the fact that the fastest growing electronics firms owe their eminence to their heavy emphasis on technical research is completely beside the point. They have vaulted to affluence on a sudden crest of unusually strong general receptiveness to new technical ideas. Also, their success has been shaped in the virtually guaranteed market of military subsidies and by military orders that in many cases actually preceded the existence of facilities to make the products. Their expansion has, in other words, been almost totally devoid of marketing effort.

Thus, they are growing up under conditions that come dangerously close to creating the illusion that a superior product will sell itself. Having created a successful company by making a superior product, it is not surprising that management continues to be oriented toward the product rather than the people who consume it. It develops the philosophy that continued growth is a matter of continued product innovation and improvement.

A number of other factors tend to strengthen and sustain this belief:

(1) Because electronic products are highly complex and sophisticated, managements become topheavy with engineers and scientists. This creates a selective bias in favor of research and production at the expense of marketing. The organization tends to view itself as making things rather than satisfying customer needs. Marketing gets treated as a residual activity, "something else" that must be done once the vital job of product creation and production is completed.

(2) To this bias in favor of product research, development, and production is added the bias in favor of dealing with controllable variables. Engineers and scientists are at home in the world of concrete things like machines, test tubes, production lines, and even balance sheets. The abstractions to which they feel kindly are those which are testable or manipulatable in the laboratory, or, if not testable, then functional, such as Euclid's axioms. In short, the managements of the new glamour-growth companies tend to favor those business activities which lend themselves to careful study, experimentation, and control—the hard, practical, realities of the lab, the shop, the books.

What gets shortchanged are the realities of the *market.* Consumers are unpredictable, varied, fickle, stupid, shortsighted, stubborn, and generally bothersome. This is not what the engineer-managers say, but deep down in their consciousness it is what they believe. And this accounts for their concentrating on what they know and what they can control, namely product research, engineering, and production. The emphasis on production becomes particularly attractive when the product can be made at declining unit costs. There is no more inviting way of making money than by running the plant full blast.

Today the top-heavy science-engineering-production orientation of so many electronics companies works reasonably well because they are pushing into new frontiers in which the armed services have pioneered virtually assured markets. The companies are in the felicitous position of having to fill, not find markets; of not having to discover what the customer needs and wants, but of having the customer voluntarily come forward with specific new product demands. If a team of consultants had been assigned specifically to design a business situation calculated to prevent the emergence and development of a customer-oriented marketing viewpoint, it could not have produced anything better than the conditions just described.

Stepchild Treatment

The oil industry is a stunning example of how science, technology, and mass production can divert an entire group of companies from their main task. To the extent the consumer is studied at all (which is not much), the focus is forever on getting information which is designed to help the oil companies improve what they are now doing. They try to discover more convincing advertising themes, more effective sales promotional drives, what the market shares of the various companies are, what people like or dislike about service station dealers and oil companies, and so forth. Nobody seems as interested in probing deeply into the basic human needs that the industry might be trying to satisfy as in probing into the basic properties of the raw material that the companies work with in trying to deliver customer satisfactions.

Basic questions about customers and markets seldom get asked. The latter occupy a stepchild status. They are recognized as existing, as having to be taken care of, but not worth very much real thought or dedicated attention. Nobody gets as excited about the customers in his own backyard as about the oil in the Sahara Desert. Nothing illustrates better the neglect of marketing than its treatment in the industry press:

> The centennial issue of the *American Petroleum Institute Quarterly,* published in 1959 to celebrate the discovery of oil in Titusville, Pennsylvania, contained 21 feature articles proclaiming the industry's greatness. Only one of these talked about its achievements in marketing, and that was only a pictorial record of how service station architecture has changed. The issue also contained a special section on "New Horizons," which was devoted to showing the magnificent role oil would play in America's future. Every reference was ebulliently optimistic, never implying once that oil might have some hard competition. Even the reference to atomic energy was a cheerful catalogue of how oil would help make atomic energy a success. There was not a single apprehension that the oil industry's affluence might be threatened or a suggestion that one "new horizon" might include new and better ways of serving oil's present customers.

> But the most revealing example of the stepchild treatment that marketing gets was still another special series of short articles on "The Revolutionary Potential of Electronics." Under that heading this list of articles appeared in the table of contents:

"In the Search for Oil"
"In Production Operations"
"In Refinery Processes"
"In Pipeline Operations"

Significantly, every one of the industry's major functional areas is listed, *except* marketing. Why? Either it is believed that electronics holds no revolutionary potential for petroleum marketing (which is more likely, and illustrates its stepchild status).

The order in which the four functional areas are listed also betrays the alienation of the oil industry from the consumer. The industry is implicitly defined as beginning with the search for oil and ending with its distribution from the refinery. But the truth is, it seems to me, that the industry begins with the needs of the customer for its products. From that primal position its definition moves steadily backstream to areas of progressively lesser importance, until it finally comes to rest at the "search for oil."

Beginning & End

The view that an industry is a customer-satisfying process, not a goods-producing process, is vital for all businessmen to understand. An industry begins with the customer and his needs, not with a patent, a raw material, or a selling skill. Given the customer's needs, the industry develops backwards, first concerning itself with the physical *delivery* of customer satisfactions. Then it moves back further to *creating* the things by which these satisfactions are in part achieved. How these materials are created is a matter of indifference to the customer, hence the particular form of manufacturing, processing, or what-have-you cannot be considered as a vital aspect of the industry. Finally, the industry moves back still further to *finding* the raw materials necessary for making its products.

The irony of some industries oriented toward technical research and development is that the scientists who occupy the high executive positions are totally unscientific when it comes to defining their companies' overall needs and purposes. They violate the first two rules of the scientific method—being aware of and defining their companies' problems, and then developing testable hypotheses about solving them. They are scientific only about the convenient things, such as laboratory and product experiments. The reason that the customer (and the satisfaction of his deepest needs) is not considered as being "the problem" is not because there is any certain belief that no such problem exists, but because an organizational lifetime has conditioned management to look in the opposite direction. Marketing is a stepchild.

I do not mean that selling is ignored. Far from it. But selling, again, is not marketing. As already pointed out, selling concerns itself with the tricks and techniques of getting people to exchange their cash for your product. It is not concerned with the values that the exchange is all about. And it does not, as marketing invariably does, view the entire business process as consisting of a tightly integrated effort to discover, create, arouse, and satisfy customer needs. The customer is somebody "out there" who, with proper cunning, can be separated from his loose change.

Actually, not even selling gets much attention in some technologically minded firms. Because there is a virtually guaranteed market for the abundant flow of their new products, they do not actually know what a real market is. It is as if they lived in a planned economy, moving their products routinely from factory to retail outlet. Their successful concentration on products tends to convince them of the soundness of what they have been doing, and they fail to see the gathering clouds over the market.

CONCLUSION

Less than 75 years ago American railroads enjoyed a fierce loyalty among astute Wall Streeters. European monarchs invested in them heavily. Eternal wealth was thought to be the benediction for anybody who could scrape a few thousand dollars together to put in rail stocks. No other form of transportation could compete with the railroads in speed, flexibility, durability, economy, and growth potentials. As Jacques Barzun put it, "By the turn of the century it was an institution, an image of man, a tradition, a code of honor, a source of poetry, a nursery of boyhood desires, a sublimest of toys, and the most solemn machine—next to the funeral hearse—that marks the epochs in man's life."[6]

Even after the advent of automobiles, trucks, and airplanes, the railroad tycoons remained imperturbably self-confident. If you had told them 60 years ago that in 30 years they would be flat on their backs, broke, and pleading for government subsidies, they would have thought you totally demented. Such a future was simply not considered possible. It was not even a discussable subject, or an askable question, or a matter which any sane person would consider worth speculating about. The very thought was insane. Yet a lot of insane notions now have matter-of-fact acceptance—for example, the idea of 100-ton tubes of metal moving smoothly through the air 20,000 feet above the earth, loaded with 100 sane and solid citizens casually drinking martinis—and they have dealt cruel blows to the railroads.

What specifically must other companies do to avoid this fate? What does customer orientation involve? These questions have in part been answered by the preceding examples and analysis. It would take another article to show in detail what is required for specific industries. In any case, it should be obvious that building an effective customer-oriented company involves far more than good intentions or promotional tricks; it involves profound matters of human organization and leadership. For the present, let me merely suggest what appear to be some general requirements.

Visceral Feel of Greatness

Obviously the company has to do what survival demands. It has to adapt to the requirements of the market, and it has to do it sooner rather than later. But mere survival is a so-so aspiration. Anybody can survive in some way or other, even the skid-row bum. The trick is to survive gallantly, to feel the surging impulse of commercial mastery; not just to experience the sweet smell of success, but to have the visceral feel of entrepreneurial greatness.

No organization can achieve greatness without a vigorous leader who is driven onward by his own pulsating *will to succeed.* He has to have a vision of grandeur, a vision that can produce eager followers in vast numbers. In business, the followers are the customers. To produce these customers, the entire corporation must be viewed as a customer-creating and customer-satisfying organism. Management must think of itself not as producing products but as providing customer-creating value satisfactions. It must push the idea (and everything it means and requires) into every nook and cranny of the organization. It has to do this continuously and with the kind of flair that excites and stimulates the people in it. Otherwise, the company will be merely a series of pigeonholed parts, with no consolidating sense of purpose or direction.

In short, the organization must learn to think of itself not as producing goods or services but as *buying customers,* as doing the things that will make people *want* to do business with it. And the chief executive himself has the inescapable responsibility for creating this environment, this viewpoint, this attitude, this aspiration. He himself must set the company's style, its direction, and its goals. This means he has to know precisely where he himself wants to go, and to make sure the whole organization is enthusiastically aware of where that is. This is a first requisite of leadership, for *unless he knows where he is going, any road will take him there.*

If any road is okay, the chief executive might as well pack his attaché case and go fishing. If an organization does not know or care where it is going, it does not need to advertise that fact with a ceremonial figurehead. Everybody will notice it soon enough.

NOTES

1. Jacques Barzun, "Trains and the Mind of Man," *Holiday,* February 1960, p. 21.
2. For more details see M. M. Zimmerman, *The Super Market: A Revolution in Distribution* (New York, McGraw-Hill Book Company, Inc., 1955), p. 48.

3. *Ibid,* pp. 45-47.
4. *The Affluent Society* (Boston, Houghton Mifflin Company, 1958), pp. 152-160.
5. Henry Ford, *My Life and Work* (New York, Doubleday, Page Company, 1923), pp. 146-147.
6. *Op cit.,* p. 20.